The observations and trees in this book were painted by the author from observations at the locations mentioned. None of the trees pictured in this book were observed or taken from other sources. The author is also the illustrator. The images are taken from actual trees or imagined trees. Any similarity to any other published image would be coincidental.

Acknowledgments

I'd like to give a big thank-you to my children for their inspiration and patience with their father on the many adventures we have shared.

Also, I wish to thank my wife for her great patience as I have personally worked through theology throughout our marriage. Thanks, too, for being a great copilot on our adventures.

Table of Contents

Introduction

A friend of mine suggested that I title this book, "Roots Too"—a humorous reference to a best-selling book entitled *Roots*. That would have been perhaps a bit misleading as to where this book was going. Another title idea was to call it, "Walking in the Woods with God." This is perhaps more to the point of where we are headed. In the woods, there are tiny insects and plants so small they require microscopic inspection and things so grand as to require a mountaintop view. Sometimes we must observe something from several vantage points before we can come close to understanding it as a whole.

"You can't see the forest for the trees." This statement seems at first to be an oxymoron. But for most of us, it is a reality in many situations in life. We find ourselves missing the big picture because the details get in the way. Our major goals in life are often obscured by the branches of day-to-day living. Many people seem to only have time in their lives to work, eat, sleep, and take out the trash.

We all aspire to stop and smell the roses, to enjoy the little pleasures of life. We all would like to succeed at our primary life goals. In this book, we will take a walk in the woods, observing not as naturalists but as learners, watching for the life's lessons we can learn from the trees.

As with each life, each tree is an individual. We will only understand the forest when we understand the individual trees. So we will look to gain insight into the purpose of the whole forest of our own lives by looking at the individual trees.

There are times when a walk in the woods will be a fearful journey with many unseen hazards. Sometimes we find ourselves caught in a briar; we may have to cut away the branches that obscure the view of our own forest. At other times, a walk in the woods is so pleasant that we get lost in the sights, sounds, and smells that we lose track of time. At times, a single breeze through the trees may seem nothing less than the very breath of God.

There were two trees of significance in Genesis—the tree of knowledge of good and evil and the tree of life. Those trees were storehouses of great things. They were trees of knowledge and wisdom—perhaps metaphorically, but I think there are things to be learned from ordinary trees. So let's explore and see—as we walk through the woods with God—what knowledge or wisdom our Creator is waiting to teach us through His trees.

CHAPTER 1

Janet's Tree

Our family and I had spent the weekend at our farm in northeast Iowa. My seven-year-old daughter was upset with her siblings and went for a walk to get away from them. After a while, it was time to load the car and head home, so I went looking for her. I searched through a couple of fields and ravines before I started to worry. I yelled for her, and finally she walked out of a thicket of pines and brush.

I asked her where she had been. With excitement in her voice, she replied, "I was playing by this really cool tree!"

Since I am always interested in cool trees, I said, "Show me."

We walked a short distance, and there, hidden behind brush and short pines, was a spectacular sight. It was a very large bur oak with huge roots coming out from the trunk nearly five feet off the ground. It looked like a giant squid with intertwining tentacles. The tree's trunk was massive, with a diameter of almost fifty inches. Its leaves and limbs above provided such great shade that the ground was almost bare. I couldn't take my eyes off those exposed roots. Some of them were nearly a foot in diameter. They were covered with the same rough bark as the limbs in the air. They were twisted; some of them merged together, forming closed circles. Many of the roots traveled ten to fifteen feet above ground before they disappeared into the dirt.

I was astonished at her find and declared, "We are now going to call this, Janet's tree."

From that point on when we went to the farm, we knew if Janet was missing, we only had to go to her tree to find her. There she would be, sitting among the roots, playing with her little figurines and toy animals.

Time has passed, and Janet is now a dentist, but that's still her tree. We put a sign—JANET'S TREE—on a small sapling growing near it. We take our friends to see it when they come to visit. For the twenty years we have known about it, the tree has never seemed to change. I visit this tree several times a year to marvel at it.

I ask visitors how they think the tree grew this way. Most people eventually come up with the right answer: water erosion exposed the roots, and over time they grew thick bark for protection. There used to be a hog lot in this area. The tree grows in a low place that eventually leads to a deep ravine. When the hogs used the area, it suffered extensive erosion. But the hogs are gone, and the tree survived. Erosion may still occur at the base as there is very little vegetation living in the dense shade, but the tree stands strong.

When I sit on the roots, I can't help but feel the power of this tree. I feel like I am sitting in the hand of God. These large roots represent His gentle yet powerful fingers. I imagine God's mighty hand gripping the earth, somehow holding it steady. Unchanging, all-powerful, gentle, casting a great shadow—God is reflected in His creation.

I find it interesting that not only are trees mentioned in the Genesis account of creation but they are mentioned twice. Special emphasis is given to the creation as God first commands it, and then the creation is realized. Then we see trees again in the Garden of Eden.

> And God said, "Let the earth put forth vegetation, plants yielding seed, and fruit trees bearing fruit in which is their seed, each according to its kind, upon the earth." And it was so. The earth brought forth vegetation, plants yielding seed according to their own kinds, and trees bearing fruit in which is their seed, each according to its kind. And God saw that it was good. (Genesis 1:11–12)

> And out of the ground the Lord God made to grow every tree that is pleasant to the sight and good for food, the tree of life also in the midst of the garden, and the tree of the knowledge of good and evil. (Genesis 2:9)

We all know what happens next. Adam and Eve eat from the forbidden tree of the knowledge of good and evil. Perhaps a fascination with trees is a dangerous thing—Adam and Eve got thrown out of the garden because of one. Actually, they were thrown out for their disobedience, not for enjoying a tree.

Generally speaking, trees are life-sustaining for humans and many other creatures here on earth. Understanding trees and promoting tree growth is a good thing. Could perhaps a tree contain knowledge? I look at very old trees and ponder the decades, maybe centuries, of seasons and changes that have happened under their branches. Our lives are so short that very old trees seem timeless. Maybe they do hold wisdom and knowledge.

Obviously, the tree of the knowledge of good and evil only existed in Eden. It's not in our backyard. I'm sure that it was a very attractive, large tree with abundant fruit. God reveals His nature in His creation.

Trees are majestic, life-giving, a gift from our Creator that reflects His power and His grip on our world. Just as Janet went to her tree as a place of refuge, so too, may we go to the hand of God for refuge.

CHAPTER 2

Signposts

Every year we paddle into the Boundary Waters Canoe Area (BWCA) in northeast Minnesota, for some fishing and time in the wilderness. Lady Boot Bay on Lac La Croix is one of my favorite spots in the BWCA, partly because it was the first place my father took me fishing when I was twelve.

There's a large, stately white pine that has stood at the entrance to Lady Boot Bay as long as I can remember. It's large enough to catch nearly everyone's eye, but not so unusual that it would cause other fishermen to comment on it. This tree is about three feet across at the base and has a significant lean out over the water that allows it to take full advantage of the sunlight. Its top stretches well above the forest canopy, and several large, lateral branches adorn the crown. The largest of these branches extends even farther out over the water, as if the tree is pointing a finger skyward at the end of a long arm. This tree has been greeting me, nearly unchanged, for all of the forty five years I've been fishing this area. It's like a signpost, welcoming me back.

There are other naturally occurring signposts I have found in my travels of the Quetico Park and BWCA wilderness complex. Rocks, waterfalls, bluffs, and other natural features guide many of my wilderness trips. Special trees tend to take on more significance for me because of their size. There is a similar large white pine that stands at the end of a mile-long paddle up Pooh Bah Creek, at the entrance to Pooh Bah Lake. This tree has an even larger and longer lateral top branch, created by storm damage, that stretches out over the water, beckoning passing adventurers.

White pines are not the predominant tree in the BWCA, but they seem to be from the water's edge since they grow so well along the shorelines. They are prized for their lumber, and many of these trees will easily live more than two hundred years. Few areas of the BWCA and Quetico Park have "old growth trees" that have been undisturbed by logging but these old growth white pines are truly spectacular.

French voyageurs in the fur-trade era used white pines to mark their paths through the lake country and to commemorate people or events. When they wanted to mark a location or commemorate an event, they would lob off the limbs of a chosen tree up to the top where the branches begin to branch out more laterally. These are called "lob pines." They have the appearance of a crown on top of a pole. These trees stood for decades, and some are still standing today.

∿

The Israelites in early Bible days also changed the landscape to commemorate an event by placing large vertical stones at the site. Usually they marked a place of remembrance of God's intervention on behalf of the Israelites. These large stones are still visible today in Israel.

After forty years of wandering in the wilderness, the moment finally came for Joshua to lead the Israelites into the Promised Land. As they crossed the Jordan River on miraculously dry land, God told them to choose twelve large stones from the middle of the riverbed and place them at their campsite that evening. Joshua 4:6–7 explains their purpose:

> When your children ask in time to come, "What do those stones mean to you?" Then you shall tell them that the waters of the Jordan were cut off before the ark of the covenant of the LORD; when it passed over the Jordan, the waters of the Jordan were cut off. So these stones shall be to the people of Israel a memorial for ever.

The sketch for this chapter is the white pine tree that welcomes me to Lady Boot Bay. It acts as a signpost for me. I look to it for guidance, to know I have arrived. Other travelers likely see it as simply another large tree. For me it stands as a sentinel, guarding the entrance to the bay. For whatever meaning I wish to attribute to this tree, it certainly triggers an emotional response for me in anticipation of the sights, sounds, and fishing about to take place, and the memories of many wonderful trips of the past.

These trees that stand as signposts to me do not carry the same significance to history as those Hebrew altars, but they carry a similar emotional significance. These seemingly timeless trees will long outlive me, and their placement along the shoreline has spiritual significance to me. God has placed them there as reassuring markers to indicate that I have arrived at my destination. They are significant for triggering my remembrance of the events of this place in my own history. Are there signposts which are significant to your life?

CHAPTER 3

Tenacity

We don't pick our parents. We have no choice as to what genes we have or where in the world we are born. It is true—one will likely have more opportunities and luxuries if born to an upper-class family in the United States than if one were born to a poor family in a remote, third-world nation.

If we compare life to a tree, life starts as a seed. As nature takes its course, the seed is blown or carried to the place where it will eventually germinate. The seed has nothing to say about where it will land. For the tree drawn for this chapter, the seed fell into a crack in a rock along a rugged lakeshore. This is not a place with good soil or nutrients. Exposure to the elements is extreme with bright, hot sun in the summer and ice and snow cover in winter. The rain washes away soil from the rock. The wind, unobstructed as it blows across the lake, hits the rock at full force. This tree exhibits tenacity. It is growing in the face of unavoidable adversity.

How do people flourish when they face great adversity? Many are born with various challenges—economic, physical, social, geographic, religious, and more. Some challenges are clearly the result of our own choices, but some are just as clearly not. Depending on where we are and what we are doing, we can expect to face some level of adversity. We are, however, not totally immovable like a tree.

Why do bad things happen to good people? This is one of the most commonly asked questions by people who doubt the Christian faith. If God is all loving, they ask, why does He allow terrible things to happen to innocent people? They assume that if God made everything, then God must be responsible for everything too—including disasters.

If God is everywhere and sees everything and is all-powerful, why doesn't He make life safe for us? A simple answer will not be satisfactory. The laws of the universe exist to maintain order within the universe. We depend on the laws of physics to be predictable. God can suspend the usual laws of physics if He chooses to do so, but He is not going to do it for our convenience, only for His purposes.

So the question remains—why do bad things happen to good people? The usual answer is that it is a question of freedom of choice. God loves us. Because of that love, He does not control our every thought and action. But if we have a choice, then logically, an alternative must exist. Something that is not *of God,* by definition would be evil. So whatever is within God's will is good, and what is not is evil. God must allow evil to exist—if only what was good and perfect existed, then we would have no choice to make. For true love to exist, there must also be a choice not to love, or we would be nothing more than robots, able only to do what our Creator chose for us. So it is out of God's love that we have the freedom to choose whether we even love our Creator. We are free to believe or not.

What does this freedom of choice have to do with our tree growing out of a slab of rock? The tree had no choice in where it grew, and because of where it is, it will never reach its full potential. We miss the spiritual truth when we look only at the result. If we evaluate a tree by its height or width or by the lumber produced from it, then this tree would be a failure. But God grew this tree where He did for a reason—maybe so that we could use it for this illustration. He is more interested in the life of the tree than the results of it growing in rock.

To apply the parable of the soils in Matthew 13 to the tree in this situation may cause us to misunderstand. Rather, the story of the man born blind, as recounted in John 9:1–34, is more appropriate here. The disciples asked Jesus why this man was born blind. People of the time believed that birth defects or disabilities were a sign of God's judgment. But Jesus answered, "It was not that this man sinned, or his parents, but that the works of God might be made manifest in him." Did you get that? This man was given his blindness so that Jesus could teach His disciples and the religious leaders of the day—and us!—a lesson. This is a mystery, but it shows us that we cannot understand the things of the spiritual world when we look only at the things of the physical world.

Just as the story of the blind man's healing leaves us astounded, the growth of this tree out of a crack in a rock is amazing, too. God reveals His glory in a tree that grows in the face of adversity. No two trees or people have the same opportunity. Each has its own circumstances to contend with. God doesn't ask who was the most successful; He asks who looked to God for answers within their circumstances.

Matthew 7:20 says, "You will know them by their fruits." The fruit that God looks for is spiritual fruit. Our small, gnarly tree is amazing, not because of its size but because of its adaptation in adversity. It doesn't grow to show off; it grows to live. When it comes to people, God is more interested in the condition of the heart than the size of a donation or the grandeur of an action. This tree embodies the idea of the poor widow putting her last coin in the offering plate.

> [41] He sat down opposite the treasury, and watched the crowd putting money into the treasury. Many rich people put in large sums. [42] A poor widow came and put in two small copper coins, which are worth a penny. [43] Then he called his disciples and said to them, "Truly I tell you, this poor widow has put in more than all those who are contributing to the treasury. [44] For all of them have contributed out of their abundance; but she out of her poverty has put in everything she had, all she had to live on." (Mark 12:41-44)

God looks for our faith, for our perseverance. We should strive not for worldly gain but for heavenly reward. Galatians 6:9–10 gives advice for perseverance.

> Let us not grow weary in well-doing, for in due season we shall reap, if we do not lose heart. So then, as we have opportunity, let us do good to all men, and especially to those who are of the household of faith.

God is not concerned with where we are planted but whether we hold fast. Like a tree growing on a solid rock, we must strive to grow toward the light that we might live and love in spite of our particular adversity.

God gave you your unique circumstances. He wants to see what you do with them. Will you seek Him out with your life, in whatever situation may arise? He wants a relationship with you. He is less concerned about how successful you are, how long you live, or how many feathers you have in your cap. Don't grow just to be the tallest tree in the forest. Grow to reach for the light of God, no matter what your circumstances are. Stand firm in your faith and know that your growth is for God's purpose and not so you can be compared to the trees around you.

CHAPTER 4

Adaptability

After a long day of paddling and portaging on a trip to Sturgeon Lake, we reached the first group of campsites there. These campsites are close to the top of the Maligne River, and there is good fishing in the currents as the water leaves Sturgeon Lake.

We call this spot the gunboat campsite. It consists mostly of a large flat rock that sticks out into the water with about a four-foot elevation off the water line. The rock looks like the prow of a ship.

Since most of the small point is solid rock, the tent sites are located farther back where the rock connects to the woods.

One of the first things I do when arriving at a campsite is look around for the best place to pitch the tent. A good tent site has level ground, sufficient space and soil to drive tent stakes, and is high enough that rain would not cause concern. As I looked for that night's tent site, I noticed a curious row of trees along the shore. The trees all looked the same—they were nearly the same diameter, all white cedar, and they were fairly evenly spaced. Each successive tree was slightly shorter than the one before it. (No, this is not a cell phone service ad.)

I went a bit closer to look and realized that they were not individual trees at all—they were actually all branches of the same tree. Early in the growth of this tree, the unstable shoreline must have caused the tree to fall over, and each of the limbs took on the characteristics of a full tree with branches hanging down in all directions, just like a normal tree would have. I marveled at the sight of this tree and thought that it was a rare occurrence.

Since then, I've found many such trees at campsites throughout the BWCA/Quetico wilderness. I now think it's not such a rare phenomenon along shorelines where ice, wind, and waves cause trees to tumble. It is a testament to the adaptability of some species to change. In this case, a tree adapted to become a mini forest of its own, taking advantage of the natural tree shape so that each of its branches could catch more sunlight.

Most organisms have some ability to adapt. Taking advantage of opportunities to survive and grow is part of life. This tree is taking advantage of what was not such a good thing—falling over. But this tree, in its fall, found it could cover more ground and collect more sunlight than it ever would have standing upright. It accepted its change and made the most of it.

Many books have been written about change. Change is, in a sense, the process of adapting. Businesses strive to implement positive change in product lines in order to gain competitive advantage. Even in the woods, a tree gains a competitive advantage if it's able to adapt to its environment. In business, there is often strong resistance to change. People protest, saying "But we've always done it this way." If your product is a fine wine, then changing to a new technique may not necessarily lead to a better product, and many businesses pride themselves on not taking shortcuts. However, if you are selling cell phones and you are happy with the status quo, you will soon be out of business.

We are creatures of habit and we tend to be resistant to change, sometimes without even knowing why. We have friends we know well and with whom we are comfortable, and so we like to keep our same friends. We find a favorite dish at a restaurant and find ourselves ordering "I'll have the usual."

Few people generated more change in the world than Jesus Christ. He met much resistance from the Jewish leadership, not only toward His teachings but toward His person as well. Change was difficult for His disciples.

Acts 10:10–16 tells the story of change brought about in the new church through a vision God gave Peter.

> And he became hungry and desired something to eat; but while they were preparing it, he fell into a trance and saw the heaven opened, and something descending, like a great sheet, let down by four corners upon the earth. In it were all kinds of animals and reptiles and birds of the air. And there came a voice to him, "Rise, Peter; kill and eat." But Peter said, "No, Lord; for I have never eaten anything that is common or unclean." And the voice came to him again a second time, "What God has cleansed, you must not call

common." This happened three times, and the thing was taken up at once to heaven.

Peter wondered about the meaning of the dream, but did not understand until he met Cornelius, a Roman centurion. In Acts 10:34–38, Peter adapts his ways because of that dream and presents the gospel to the Gentiles for the first time.

> And Peter opened his mouth and said: "Truly I perceive that God shows no partiality, but in every nation any one who fears him and does what is right is acceptable to him. You know the word which he sent to Israel, preaching good news of peace by Jesus Christ (he is Lord of all), the word which was proclaimed throughout all Judea, beginning from Galilee after the baptism which John preached: how God anointed Jesus of Nazareth with the Holy Spirit and with power; how he went about doing good and healing all that were oppressed by the devil."

As Peter continued speaking, the Holy Spirit came upon them and they were saved. In Acts 11:18, we read the final proclamation of the change that was brought about by Peter's dream, as the apostles declare, "Then to the Gentiles also God has granted repentance unto life."

Until this point, the church had centered its early life in Jerusalem among Jews who had converted to Christianity. Because of this vision and despite resistance among the brethren (Acts 11:2–3), Peter worked hard to open the church to the Gentiles as well as the Jews. Where would we be if he had not adapted?

As Christians we never arrive to perfection in this life. We are in a constant state of change. In Philippians 3:12–14, the Apostle Paul encourages us to actively move forward through life.

Not that I have already obtained this or am already perfect; but I press on to make it my own, because Christ Jesus has made me his own. Brethren, I do not consider that I have made it my own; but one thing I do, forgetting what lies behind and straining forward to what lies ahead, I press on toward the goal for the prize of the upward call of God in Christ Jesus.

We are not always comfortable with change, but with it we can grow, adapt, and strive to be better, to perhaps become more like Christ. To do this, we must embrace what is unfamiliar, what is uncomfortable, and people we don't yet know.

An unfortunate event—like that tree falling over—can become the change that is the beginning of something better.

CHAPTER 5

God's Calling Card

Our family was enjoying a trip into the wilderness for solitude and fishing. Four days earlier, we had been shuttled to our first portage by a canoe outfitter. We were now well into the Boundary Waters Canoe Area and twenty-five miles from the nearest road. The last eight miles we had traveled were paddle-only waters.

The original itinerary called for us to move camp closer to the pick-up point for the last day. However, we decided to stay at our more remote campsite one last night to have more time for better quality fishing. Staying this last night at our primary camp would eliminate having to tear down and set up one more time. Weather seemed to be in our favor for good traveling in the morning, so we all agreed to stay put one more night.

I poked my head out of my tent the next morning at daybreak, knowing we had several miles to travel. I was a little disturbed to see an ethereal gray haze permeating the forest. We had planned to break camp before 7:00 a.m., for a noon pick-up time with the out-fitters. We had almost four hours of travel time to the pick-up point.

We packed quickly, but as I looked out across the lake, dense fog continued to partially obscure the view of the islands across from our camp. The sun was not visible, but by the time on my watch, I was sure that it was well after sunrise. On any other misty morning, I would have sat around the fire, warming my hands on a cup of cocoa while I waited for the sun to break through. But on this day, I felt that we were obligated to cross the lake—even with the risk of getting lost.

Navigating the lakes in a fog is dangerous because it is very easy to become disoriented. Some even consider navigating the islands and bays difficult in broad daylight. Distances are hard to judge, and it's easy to think you're traveling in a straight line, but in actuality you might be making a slow turn. Many of the islands look identical. Crooked Lake is a couple of miles across in some places and over eighteen miles from end to end.

As we crossed Crooked Lake in our canoes, we found the fog getting worse, not better. It was as if the contrast knob on an old TV had been slowly turned the wrong way. I kept my eyes glued to the map, and we picked our way, island by island, until we reached a large open area of water. I was about to head toward shore to keep from traveling in circles, but as we stopped paddling for a moment, we heard the faint sound of a waterfall. Curtain Falls was the first portage on our way out. We turned our canoes toward the sound, and for the next forty-five minutes we paddled silently as the sound of the falls grew steadily louder. Without that pause to rest and get our bearings, the sounds of the waves and our paddling would have obscured the sound of the falls, and we would have missed our portage.

At the time, I thought that navigating by the sound of a waterfall was rather unique. I knew God had made our path straight by a small miracle. And then I remembered the guidance the Israelites had received from God in their escape from Egypt:

> And the Lord went before them by day in a pillar of cloud to lead them along the way, and by night in a pillar of fire to give them light, that they might travel by day and by night; the pillar of cloud by day and the pillar of fire by night did not depart from before the people. (Exodus 13:21–22)

As we made our way safely onto the next lake, called Iron Lake, the fog began to lift. By this point, we could see well enough to navigate by sight, and we marveled at God's direction that had allowed us to be on time to meet the boat pick-up that would take us the rest of the way home. With maybe a mile to go, we were nearing the end of our paddling. We were now paddling silently out of habit. My attention was drawn to the shoreline as if there had been a noise. I caught sight of a small tree on the shoreline and then turned around to realize that everyone else was staring at it too.

I reached for my camera without saying a word, and two other members of our party said, "Hey, look, a cross!" We all easily recognized it as a cross—it was not a situation that required imagination. It was a young maple tree just starting to turn fall colors. The subtle reds and yellows of the maple sapling stood out in stark contrast to the deep greens of the conifers behind it. The tree's slender central trunk was covered in leaves and had two matched horizontal branches.

Some people have the gift of faith. God has given them the ability to comprehend His ways, and the spiritual world is readily open to them. To them, believing in Heaven, believing that Jesus is God, and trusting that His resurrection is personally redemptive are easy and self-evident beliefs. They often see miracles in everyday life and feel the Holy Spirit's presence almost continuously.

I'm not from Missouri, but I have a more "show me" approach to life and matters of faith. There are times when God can seem nonexistent for me. But matters of faith cannot be shown in a scientific experiment. By definition, faith is unseen, but it can be reasoned or explained to us so that we may find faith. We must receive faith as a gift from God. Sometimes God shows Himself in a way that is obvious to us but not to others. Our little cross tree, to me, was an obvious sign from God that His hand had been guiding us that morning. Faith develops when we open our hearts and minds to receive faith from God. It grows when we open our eyes to look for those little moments when God intervenes for us.

For me, this special little maple was God's calling card. It reminded me to be thankful to God for our good fortune and safe passage that morning. I was grateful to our Creator for the opportunities to enjoy His creation on our last fishing trip of the year. It was a reminder to thank God for holding our hands and leading us back home.

Chapter 6

Seeds of Faith

Our vacation to the Boundary Waters Canoe Area was over, and I had returned to work. I found myself thinking a lot about the cross tree we had just seen. I kept wondering how it related to faith. Faith is a belief in something that cannot be seen. Faith is belief, but it's a belief that requires action. I believed that God used the tree to help us back to town, but was that faith?

Faith is a belief with action. What action? James 2:17 says that, "Faith by itself, if it has no works, is dead." I found myself wondering if I had ever really stepped out in faith in response to something I believed. The Holy Spirit replied to my questions as a quiet thought. Are you doing anything that could have results that would not be seen in this lifetime?

I thought about that for a while. I was back to civilization, home, and work, but that weekend I decided to put some spare time into planting some trees on our property. As I worked, I realized that tree planting is definitely an act of faith. When I plant a tree, I am trusting that the effort will benefit future generations.

Tree planting on forest land may seem a waste of time, because the natural growth of trees should bring back trees where they have been cut or blown down. This would be true if our cutting were done in such a way that proper seed trees were left to repopulate the forest with diversity and good trees for future harvest.

In the Midwest, however, tree harvests of the past have not typically been done with the best interests of future generations in mind. High quality oak, shagbark hickory, and walnut have been widely harvested, while less desirable species such as elm, bitternut hickory, ironwood, and box elder have been left behind. The box elder quickly takes hold in sunlit areas. In areas with less sunlight, bitternut hickory grows up where quality oaks were harvested. Shade-tolerant species like hickory and maple take over where red and white oaks once existed. The loss of oaks reduces the presence of mast—the acorns and edible seeds that feed deer and turkeys.

Much of the focus of forest management in Midwestern forests today is to encourage growth of oaks, both for the benefit of wildlife and to reverse the ill effects of the previous selective cutting that left those less desirable trees to take over. Think of it like having a garden with good plants and weeds. If you continually pick the good flowers and leave behind the weeds, eventually all you will have is weeds.

Our forests now need a bit of weeding and planting to reverse the loss of some important species due to two centuries of cutting the "flowers." So the hope is that planting oak and walnut in open areas in the woods will restore the quality our forests once had, all for the benefit of wildlife and people in future generations.

How much faith does it require to plant trees? The year we encountered that cross-shaped tree was a year like many others. I was doing a large tree planting on our property and had gathered plenty of seed and seedlings, of both walnut and oak. I realized that it takes a measure of faith that when a seed is planted, it will escape predators to become a mature tree. It takes faith that this seed will grow to a tree to do all the things that we expect and want it do—provide home for animals, shade, convert carbon dioxide to oxygen, and perhaps become lumber. Lumber is the main purpose for which I plant trees, and one which will benefit a future generation that doesn't exist yet. Trees generally live longer than we do. A red oak takes roughly eighty years, and a walnut tree takes nearly a hundred years in our area to reach harvestable size. Best quality walnut requires more like a hundred twenty or a hundred thirty years. I will never live long enough to see these trees become lumber. There is no way I can know who will harvest these trees, or if the world will even continue to exist as it is now. But I have faith that it will happen.

Planting a seed of faith also requires a willingness to make a difference for the future with little or no likely opportunity to see the benefit in this life. Many Christians fail to plant spiritual seed toward future growth. This is, of course, vital for Christianity's continued existence. Just as a forest without seeds is one generation from extinction, Christianity without people sharing their faith is one generation from obscurity.

Even though faith is simply belief, that belief has power. In Mathew 17:20, Jesus explains how powerful faith can be when used in alignment with God's will.

> "Truly, I say to you, if you have faith as a grain of mustard seed, you will say to this mountain, 'Move from here to there,' and it will move; and nothing will be impossible to you."

This passage is a difficult passage for some because they get stuck on the mountain and miss the concept of faith. If so many people have faith, they wonder, why don't we see all kinds of mountains being moved around? I believe that Jesus is referring to the spiritual world, invisible to us because we see with our physical eyes and do not look with spiritual eyes. When we look for the spiritual world, we can see the action of God and the faith-filled acts of believers.

It takes some faith, and it takes a willingness to do something right, to plant seeds of faith for those who follow us. Planting a tree or a spiritual seed may help your great-grandchildren or a future generation you will never meet. Many people with faith ask, "Why bother? Christ will return soon and make a new earth and a new Jerusalem." This could happen soon, but we don't know when. Doing something now that is right for the future is an act of faith. Some would say we don't need to evangelize because faith is given from God, or they might say that it is the job of professional ministers of the faith to spread the word. Faith in God's creation and what we do for others now or in the future is work worth doing.

Similarly, we must tend to the faith of others as stewards of what we have been given for the benefit of future generations. Planting seeds, spiritual or otherwise, is an act of faith that springs from the hope of a future worth dreaming about. When we plant tree seeds, there may be thousands lost, but one of those acorns may become a giant oak. When we plant spiritual seeds, we should scatter them far and wide because we cannot know what may grow. Paul taught and planted seeds across the Roman Empire. Those seeds grew in ways that we can still observe today. If you have a measure of faith, give it a chance to grow and plant some seeds.

CHAPTER 7

Impermeable

Many of the canoe routes I take through Minnesota and Ontario are historical travel routes used by Native Americans and French voyageurs. They traveled the rivers by canoe because the many exposed rocks and marshes of the land made travel quite difficult. I have found that paddling a canoe along the river slows things down to a point that it is possible to study an individual tree along the shore. If I were motoring by in a speedboat, I would not have the opportunity to study an individual tree, at least not for very long.

The shortest distance between two points is a straight line, and I adhere to that theory in my canoe. Sometimes I find myself waiting for other canoes in our group because they choose to travel in a less efficient, unconventional, zigzag route. The increased distance they travel sometimes gives me the time to study something along the shoreline in more detail and sometimes take a picture.

This straight-line approach on Tanner Lake always takes me close to the north shoreline. One stretch of it takes me right up to the tips of the overhanging trees. The first time I traveled that route, I discovered several white cedars bending out over the lake, growing right at the water's edge.

On later trips, I realized that these trees could tolerate being under floodwaters without dying. But I also noticed that many of the lower limbs were devoid of needles. White-cedar needles are more like flattened stems that give the tree a fernlike appearance. The lower branches spend the winter under layers of snow and sometimes remain under water in the spring. Because of this, the trees don't show any green for the first several feet off the ground.

With my first observation of these trees, I was aware that sometimes they reached so far out over the lake that their trunks actually curved under the water. I figured that I was either seeing the trees at high water and that shortly they would be exposed, or the tree would be dead the next time I came by.

After nearly two decades of paddling by the same point, it is now apparent to me that these trees have virtually never changed. Even in normal water levels, a few of these trees' trunks are underwater, but the end of the tree is still alive. Some of the trunks are nearly always underwater, yet the exposed branches do not die. Most other types of trees will die if the trunk is submerged in water for long periods of time. These trees didn't grow much; in fact, the growth is so slow that I have not observed notable change over decades.

It stands to reason that the rocks I pass on certain points or islands would be the same one year to the next; it's a fact that I use them as landmarks along the shore. But trees? These white cedars are more like rocks than trees. They are unchanging and quite distinctive, always there, year after year. These white cedars are perhaps some of the oldest trees in the north woods, reaching several hundred years of age. Their height would be dwarfed by much larger and younger white pines and Norway pines, but the white northern cedar has figured out a way to live where other pines would have died.

What makes them able to withstand the same effects of water that causes other trees to die? The answer is, they are impermeable. The bark of the trunk forms a barrier to water. If water permeates the tree, then the flow of sap up the tree stops, and nutrients are taken away by dissolution and dilution. But the trees I travel by on the edge of Tanner Lake have been standing there for hundreds of years, much of the time partially underwater.

Many times in our lives, it pays to have thick skin. We must learn the difficult lesson not to allow hurtful words to bother us. We must learn to distinguish between words of instruction and constructive criticism and words of malcontent, spoken to the detriment of others.

Many have hurt others within the guise of giving constructive criticism. Some with smiles on their faces and a welcoming handshake will penetrate defenses only to inflict great damage. Motives are nearly impossible to judge from a singular view, and by mistake we may assign motives to words that were said innocently. Determining whether a person's approach is genuinely friendly or ultimately manipulative can be challenging.

People talk about perspective or being able to see something from multiple viewpoints. Try as we may, it is difficult to see things as others see them. When we try to see things from a third-person point of view, we often color that perception with our own assumptions of the motives of others. It would be charitable and perhaps healthier to put the best construction on others' motives so as to reduce our chances of misunderstanding or being hurt by words not intended to do so.

Some words may be spoken with the intent to hurt the listener. Regardless, the lesson remains that we can keep growing and living even in harsh environments if we have some protection from outside forces. Some will develop that thick skin, while others will avoid contact and conversation as a way of hiding themselves away. But we can still grow in a hostile environment if we develop a sort of personal impermeability.

Living and growing in the midst of potential harm is not easy. Think of the Christian life. We might decide to live a Christian life of solitude. This monastic existence would be relatively free of risk from harm by others. However, it would be difficult to help others if we have little interaction with those who suffer.

We could also choose to live a more missionary-type life by living among and helping others who are in need. For a life to remain Christ like, there must be some impermeability to the damaging influences that surround us. Negative influences from others that could cause temptations or hurt feelings may be mitigated by the Holy Spirit in our lives.

We observe the unflappable individual who seems always able to do the right thing in the midst of chaos without fear of being harmed. This individual may be impermeable to the damage through Christ's strength in their life. Faith in God and care for others through the Holy Spirit will soften the blow from another's harsh words.

If we are willing to take the risk, we can empathize or understand the other person's perspective. Tell them what you heard them say and ask them why they feel the way they do. This will perhaps open the doors of communication to understanding which may in turn lead to reconciliation.

Paul says, "Take the whole armor of God, that you may be able to withstand in the evil day, and having done all, to stand" (Ephesians 6:13). Christian faith allows us to go into danger, not recklessly, but with the assurance that we have God's hand of protection and His love, regardless of the outcome. We can withstand harsh words knowing that we are the cherished children of God, which no one can devalue.

A tree impermeable to water may live in wet conditions not tolerated by other trees. We can survive harsh social environments if we receive the Holy Spirit as our guide to our words and actions. The Spirit in our lives will protect us from pressures of the world that could destroy us spiritually.

Chapter 8

Chains and Cables

Crooked Lake is one of my favorite lakes in the Quetico wilderness of Ontario. Our family has visited this lake on numerous canoe trips. It's a great place to fish. We often camp near a place called Saturday Bay. Crooked Lake straddles the US-Canadian border, so the northern half is in Canada, and the southern half is in the United States.

One of the best fishing spots that I've found on this lake is about a hundred yards from the tree I sketched for this chapter. This Norway pine grows among many others of its species in the area and is not unusual in its size. What is unusual about this tree is the old logging cable that's attached to its base. There are other areas in the BWCA and Quetico National Park that show evidence of prior logging, but most of that stopped in 1946, when these two areas were set aside for recreation. This rusty remnant of cable is similar to what we have found in other areas of the park. In some places we've found iron rings cemented to rocks that were used for tethers to hold logs for transportation. On Pooh Bah Creek, there are remnants of a sluice used to direct logs down the creek from a holding area. Most of the cables and rings that still exist are in areas where logs were gathered together before they were moved through creeks or rapids. Occasionally, we find a bit of chain, but cable is more common.

This particular tree that is wrapped with cable is showing its age because the top of the tree is now dying. Although it isn't a huge tree, the rocky site that it grows on is rather harsh, and the tree probably grew very slowly. I have been aware of this tree for over ten years, and I've been unable to detect any change in it. This is simply a reflection of the slow growth and the long time it takes to grow large trees in harsh environments.

These pieces of chain and cable can be used as metaphors for things of the past that still hold onto us. Bad experiences, injuries, and wounds that don't heal may hold us back from future growth. Consider Paul's words in Philippians 3:13–14:

> I do not consider that I have made it my own; but one thing I do, forgetting what lies behind and straining forward to what lies ahead, I press on toward the goal for the prize of the upward call of God in Jesus Christ.

Paul encourages us to let go of the past and to concentrate on pressing forward to the future. Some forms of counseling are based on understanding a person's childhood or past. Understanding one's past may give insight as to the causes of or propensity toward certain problems. However, we must not wallow in the past or allow it to prevent us from moving forward.

Forgiveness is important for both the forgiven and the forgiver. If you have been wronged by someone in the past, it is important that you forgive that person—even if they don't recognize that they wronged you, and even if they don't ask for forgiveness. If you hold a grudge because of the insult to you, this will be a chain to your past. Realistically, we may not always be able to forget the past, and remembering those things that hurt us may prevent us from being hurt in the future. However, we cannot hold onto our anger or pain in a way that hobbles us from moving on. Consider the advice given in Hebrews 12:1–2:

> Therefore, since we are surrounded by so great a cloud of witnesses, let us also lay aside every weight, and sin which clings so closely, and let us run with perseverance the race that is set before us, looking to Jesus the pioneer and perfecter of our faith, who for the joy that was set before him endured the cross, despising the shame, and is seated at the right hand of the throne of God.

A tree hobbled by a cable has little choice but to continue to grow the best that it can. Some difficulties in life can be moved away from while others that we cannot move away from must be endured. Like this tree on the shores of Crooked Lake, however, we should not let our past stop us from growing into the future.

CHAPTER 9

Cedars of Lebanon

The logging industry has been the center of controversy for generations. The Pacific Northwest has been a battleground over big trees. There is much to protect. The spotted owl is a focal point of protecting old-growth forests in the Pacific Northwest. The spotted owl is not completely unique as a creature; there are many types of owls. But what makes this owl the poster child in the debate is that the spotted owl's favorite habitat is old-growth forest. To understand the controversy of the spotted owl is to understand that this is an argument not simply to protect the owl but to address the larger problem of ecosystem loss.

Old-growth forest is really the issue. When an old-growth forest is cut, the type and quality of trees that are lost will not be replaced for centuries. We have been cutting old-growth forest since the Pilgrims arrived in New England, and now we're to the point that only a few old-growth forests remain.

John Muir was perhaps the most famous protector of wild lands and old-growth forests in our country. He was one of the earliest champions of the cause. Many people in the eastern half of the United States mistakenly believe his was a cause to protect the giant Sequoias and redwoods from destruction. Certainly, those are very much prized trees due to their magnificent size. But what many don't understand is that old growth can be present in a large variety of species.

In the Pacific Northwest, the western hemlocks and Douglas fir old-growth forests are also spectacular in size and age. Because these areas don't contain redwoods, however, many old-growth stands of Douglas fir or western hemlock are still being cut to satisfy our needs for lumber, furniture, and wood products. In the Midwest, most of the old-growth forests were cut long ago, and there are only a few small patches left. In the BWCA, there are still a few spots that contain giant white pines that have never been cut. There are even fewer hardwood old-growth forests, and many times they're hard to even imagine.

On a visit to Mammoth Cave in Kentucky, my wife and I sent our children on a just-for-kids spelunking tour. The kids were given plastic hardhats and kneepads, and they got to crawl through narrow places in Mammoth Cave. I love caves and I, of course, was jealous, but we had toured other parts of the cave earlier in the day. While we waited for the kid's tour to finish, my wife and I took a short walk aboveground. We wandered the hills overlying the cave, and to my astonishment, we found huge hardwoods—oaks with trunks so large it would take two or three people to encircle them with their arms. These gigantic trees had been protected from logging by the presence of the cave beneath their roots. This patch of trees allowed me to see what our forests looked like to the early settlers.

One of my favorite hikes is an easy one in Glacier National Park called the Trail of the Cedars. It leads to Avalanche Lake. The trail meanders along a small creek that comes from Avalanche Lake. This ground is a moist lowland area protected from winds and the forces of nature, and it's ideal for the magnificent stand of white cedars.

Standing beneath these trees is like standing in a cathedral so grand as to be unmatched by St. Peter's Basilica in Rome. The architects who built St. Peter's Basilica wanted worshippers to feel the presence and power of God. In much the same way, I feel the presence of God standing under these immense old-growth trees.

You can't eat these trees. You can't even climb them. They are so tall, I can't even break off a limb. They blot out the sun. They block the wind. They shade the ground so that only mosses survive. The love I have for these forests is a feeling that defies my own explanation. I'm simply drawn to them to stare up at the glory of God's creation.

In the Bible, there are several references to the cedars of Lebanon. In Ezekiel 31:2–3, Egypt's greatness is compared to the cedar in Lebanon.

> Whom are you like in your greatness? Behold, I will liken you to a cedar in Lebanon, with fair branches and forest shade, and of great height, its top among the clouds.

We look on old-growth forest with awe. Perhaps more importantly, we look upon them in humility, seeing them as the hand of God and respecting them, protecting them; keeping mindful that we are often disrespectful of the creation God has laid before us.

CHAPTER 10

Beams!

We had reached the inn at Yellowstone. The large double doors were bordered by massive tree trunks. I held one door as my three kids filed through. The logs surrounding the door were painted brown, but they still had that just-cut-from-the-woods look. The branches had been cut flush to the logs and the bark removed, but they were otherwise fully round tree trunks, spectacular in size.

We advanced as a group into the crowd of people inside. We made our way through the foyer and into the great room. Our gaze was sucked skyward by the grand amount of space crisscrossed with huge logs.

I looked at my kids, smiled big, and exclaimed, "Beams!"

Having heard me say this many times before, they looked at me with disapproval, shook their heads, and just said disdainfully, "Dad."

The great room of the Old Faithful Inn is well known to many travelers. They come to Yellowstone to marvel at God's handiwork, but if there is anything man-made in all of Yellowstone Park that would be called a must-see, I believe Old Faithful Inn is it.

My kids have experienced this brief conversation in countless places. From my cousin's original log cabin in Pennsylvania to Many Glaciers Lodge in Montana to our cabin in Minnesota, the word "beams" has been exclaimed with special meaning in our family. Now when we walk into a building that has great beams, I simply point up, and my kids say, "beams."

Perhaps the two most important beams in history are sketched for this chapter. In Latin, the beam permanently fixed to the ground is called a *stipes*. The cross piece that Jesus carried partway to Calvary is called the *patibulum*.

There is much written about how exactly the crossbeam was attached to the upright for Christ's crucifixion. Most historians believe that the crossbeam was set on top of the stipes to form a T shape. Perhaps the sign saying, "This is Jesus of Nazareth, the King of the Jews" was nailed above His head. The sign was carried in the procession to Calvary. This sign could have completed the shape of a cross. Or perhaps Jesus' head completed the shape of the cross.

Though the debate goes on, the shape of the cross is really an unimportant detail. It is what happened at the cross that day that's important. Two things happened at the same time. A previously little-known carpenter of Galilee allowed Himself to be killed without protest through crucifixion. And in the same moment, the Creator of the universe willingly sacrificed Himself wholly and personally for you and me, so that we may have a sacrificial, loving, eternal relationship with Him.

If Jesus' death on the cross has no relevance to a given person whatsoever, then it follows that the Bible contains only historical texts and moral lessons. However, Jesus' death was more than the unfortunate sentence of a philosopher. His was the death of the heir of the universe, and we and the generations before and after us are responsible for His death. Therefore, we must consider His words as walking orders for ordering our personal lives.

My wife, daughter, and I toured Israel. The Via Dolorosa, or Way of Sorrows, is traveled daily by thousands as a symbolic reenactment of Jesus' trip to the cross. If you watch the crowds, you may see people actually carrying homemade crosses to honor Jesus. The precise beginning and end of Jesus' path may be in question, but that did not concern us—we just wanted to walk the streets that Jesus did on His way to Calvary. So we walked the Via Dolorosa.

Halfway along this crowded street, one of the members of our tour tripped off a curb and badly sprained her ankle. She couldn't put weight on it, so the members of our group tried to help. We had several blocks to go to get to a vehicle, as this area was a walking-only portion of Jerusalem. We walked on either side of her, supporting her weight. We tried a two-person carry with one person on each side, but she kept losing her grip and falling. I suggested that I try carrying her like a portage pack. I was accustomed to carrying heavy packs on portage trips, so I had her get behind me, wrap her arms around my neck, and hold on. It was rather easy to lift her weight by simply leaning forward. Our whole tour followed along until we reached a cab to take her to the hospital.

This sight drew more attention than the occasional tourist with a cross. In retrospect, I realized that this occurrence at that moment and place was not coincidental, but a clear message to me. I am reminded of Simon of Cyrene in Matthew 27:32. "As they went out, they came upon a man of Cyrene, Simon by name; this man they compelled to carry his cross." Simon was compelled to carry Jesus' cross when Jesus no longer could.

This act by Simon was an act of service to Jesus even if the Roman soldiers did command it. Perhaps Simon was a follower of Jesus; perhaps he just happened to be standing there. We don't know. But whatever the circumstances, he was asked to share in Jesus' burden. Simon carried this beam for Christ.

If we look, we can see ourselves in the roles of all who were present. When we tell a white lie, it's as if we are part of the crowd yelling, "release Barabbas." Matthew 27:22 tells us that the *whole crowd* demanded, "Let him be crucified." And when Pilate refused responsibility for His death, the people answered, "His blood be on us and on our children" (Matthew 27:25). In those words, we and all generations since were implicated as responsible for Jesus' death by the crowd in Jerusalem that day.

To understand the act of Jesus' crucifixion, we need to see ourselves there—as part of the crowd, a flogging Roman soldier, a Pharisee, or perhaps Simon. By our nature, we betray Jesus. We attack Him, accuse Him, and even help Him on His way to crucifixion. If we understand these actions as if they were our own, we can understand more fully Christ's sacrifice. It was our sins that He accepted. He took them quietly, willingly, lovingly. Even today, He persistently takes all that we personally can dish out. Jesus' act is analogous to a parent tolerating the kicking, screaming, rejection of an injured child who is inconsolably hurting.

Perhaps we need to understand the crucifixion from Simon's viewpoint. Maybe there is a beam that we need to pick up and carry. Even if it wasn't our task to carry that beam and we don't know why we were singled out to carry it, we need to do so. We share in the burden of pain, and we too may need to quietly, willingly, lovingly tolerate the anger, pain, and retaliation from those who are wounded.

Is there a beam you need to pick up and carry?

CHAPTER 11

Paradise

When I see a picture of a palm tree at water's edge, I think of paradise. Many people dream of a break from winter's grip to get away to warm sands and beach chairs.

We think of relaxation, vacation, perhaps umbrella drinks. Here in the Midwest, there are several months of the year when it is too cold to enjoy being outdoors, so it is a pleasant thought—the warm sun on your skin and the feel of hot sand on your feet.

Of course, not everyone dreams of going to the beach when they see a palm tree. But for many, the sight of the palm tree brings memories of coconut suntan lotion, the fun of water sports, and sitting on a beach with a book through a peaceful afternoon.

We call these folks "snowbirds." Snowbirds are Northerners who travel to some southern destination to avoid the snow. Not all of them hit the beach. Most are simply looking for warmer climates to avoid the winter weather.

My wife and I often take midwinter trips. Hawaii is a favorite destination. Sometimes I daydream about what life would be like, living on a private tropical island with no time schedule and no worries. On one such trip, I was sitting in my beach chair and noticed a coconut lying on the beach.

I looked at it and thought to myself, "I could just pick up coconuts on the beach and fish in the surf and be happy with the simple life." So I picked up the coconut and gave it a good shake. If a coconut is still good, you can hear the milk splash around inside when you shake it. If there's no sound, the milk may have leaked out through a crack or just dried out.

This particular coconut looked fresh and had a good splash sound, so I decided to try to break it open. No saw, no knife, but oh, this is supposed to be the simple life right? So I carried it along the beach until I found a good, solid chunk of lava-rock. I threw the coconut against the rock for a good long while, and after many throws the husk finally came off. The husk is rather fibrous and thick, but a person with persistence can get it off. What is left is a round, brown ball.

This brown ball is what contains the coconut meat. So with a few more whacks on the rock and a couple of scrapes on my hand, I succeeded in getting it open. The ball broke into about a half-dozen pieces. The milk spilled onto the sand and several pieces of coconut meat went into the sand as well. But I had a couple of pieces of coconut meat with brown bark still clinging to them that I could eat. It had taken half an hour, but I was finally able to sample fresh coconut meat.

It tasted okay, but it was not as good as the caramelized coconut candy sold at the roadside vegetable stands. That coconut is sweet and a bit chewy. Fresh coconut is harder and slightly bitter. I had the satisfaction of success, but after all my hard work and a scraped hand, I decided that it was much easier to keep my day job and buy the shredded coconut they sell in the store.

When we use the word "paradise," we usually think of somewhere like Hawaii or better yet, the Garden of Eden—a beautiful place where all of our needs are perfectly met. But Jesus spoke of a different paradise. The translation of the word he used is more along the lines of a walled courtyard garden, one protected from the outside. From the cross, Jesus declares salvation for the penitent thief dying next to Him.

> [39] One of the criminals who were hanged railed at him, saying, "Are you not the Christ? Save yourself and us!" [40] But the other rebuked him, saying, "Do you not fear God, since you are under the same sentence of condemnation? [41] And we indeed justly; for we are receiving the due reward of our deeds; but this man has done nothing wrong." [42] And he said, "Jesus, remember me when you come into your kingdom." [43] And he said to him, "Truly, I say to you, today you will be with me in Paradise." (Luke 23:39-43)

These words should strike us to the bone. I can guarantee you, that thief knew his actions would disqualify him from heaven. But with a simple confession, Christ changed his future, his eternity. We are like that penitent thief, pleading for mercy in our last hour. Our lives are short. Each sin separates us from God, no matter how big or little we think it is. As much as we work at being good, we can never be good enough to earn our way into the presence of God. We need help to be admitted to paradise. Adam and all his descendants were cast out of the Garden of Eden for disobedience. Some think that if we work hard at doing good things, then maybe God will have mercy on us and take us in. This is called "works righteousness."

Nearly all religions of the world are founded on this works-righteousness idea. Even many Christians think that they have to clean up their own lives by working hard to gain God's favor. But doing this is to misunderstand the good news Jesus gives us. The gospel explains what it means to have a friend in high places, a backstage pass, a "fast pass" that lets us skip the long line for admission.

In Disneyland, you can get a fast pass for a ride that has a long line so that you can do other things rather than wait in line. When it's your appointed time, you can show up and get directly on the ride. With Christ you can know right now what your future is. You can get a fast pass; you need not be left wondering if you were nice enough to others to get in. You don't have to wait till the end of your life for the punch line. Assurance is granted, free.

We have all been offered something "for free," only to discover that there are strings attached. The free item is given with the purchase of another item, perhaps. But admission to the kingdom of God is free with no strings attached. You don't have to dress yourself up, you don't have to bring anything—you just come as you are.

If we accept that we have rebelled and are not perfect, if we know that Christ died for us and tell others of Him, we get the free pass to the party. Romans 10:9 says, "if you confess with your lips that Jesus is Lord and believe in your heart that God raised him from the dead, you will be saved."

Pride is the main thing that separates us from God. We are often unwilling to admit our faults and our own insignificance and our desire to be independent rather than dependent on our Heavenly Father. But Christ is waiting, holding our ticket, that fast pass to grant us admission into paradise.

Jesus invites us to join Him in paradise. No waiting in line—like the thief on the cross, we can know today that we will join Him there. We don't know what tomorrow will bring. We strive all day long. We work hard to make money to be able to spend a week on the beach. If we will turn our lives over to Christ, we can be in paradise without the airline ticket. He invites us to join Him, without work on our part.

Put on your sunglasses and hat, and head for the light. Let's go sit under a palm tree. Let's go to paradise! I will be sad if you won't come too.

CHAPTER 12

Independent, Dependent, or Interdependent

Walking through the woods, you will come across a variety of organisms growing on the trees. There are various mosses, lichens, vines, and other vegetation that depend on trees for their survival. Many animals make their homes and nests on or within trees. Symbiotic organisms need each other to survive. One organism supplies a need of the other. Symbiotic organisms, like insects that help with pollination, provide benefit to the trees. They live in trees to the mutual benefit of the tree and the organism.

Parasitic (dependent) organisms, on the other hand, take something from the other organism without helping it in return. Successful parasitic organisms, like insects that feed upon the leaves, do not help the host tree, but rarely do they eat more leaves than the host can handle, thereby killing the tree. If the parasitic insect ate all of the leaves and killed the tree, then the insects would literally eat themselves out of house and home.

Some organisms are both harmful and helpful. They are interdependent. Squirrels, for example, eat a tremendous number of acorns, but oak trees make more acorns than squirrels can eat, so they bury them in the ground. Inadvertently, the squirrels are planting the acorns because they don't always remember where they buried them, or they may be unable to find the acorns again beneath deep snow. Some years there are so many acorns that the squirrels cannot eat them all. In lean years when there aren't enough acorns to go around and few if any make it to grow new trees, the squirrel population may drop. This, in turn, lets the next bumper crop of acorns grow new trees again.

God's creation is fascinating. There are organisms that live independently with no need for one another. There are those that live dependently, such as a parasitic organism. And there are those that are interdependent, like the squirrel.

Trees are strong, independent organisms and would seem to be something to emulate metaphorically as an honorable life. A life well-rooted, serving others, producing food, and leaving a legacy of fine lumber. However, our lives may be best lived if we are interdependent, rather than dependent or independent. Now, I realize this statement may seem paradoxical. As children we are taught to be independent, and some like that because it implies freedom. Some like to be dependent because they see it as safer. But interdependence requires interaction with others in a give-and-take, preferably caring interaction.

The sketch for this chapter shows two bromeliads growing on the limb of a large tropical tree. Bromeliads collect water from rain in the throat of the plant rather than from soil. The bromeliad is dependent on the tree for a place to live. The tree is not significantly harmed by the bromeliad. The bromeliad may attract pollinators when it blooms, but it uses the tree as a support. Growing in a tree allows bromeliads a location up in the forest canopy with filtered light and just enough moisture to thrive.

There are times in our lives when we are more like parasites than other times. During these times, we are highly dependent on the abundance of others. For instance, as infants we are completely dependent on our parents. The same can also be true when we are of advanced age, perhaps near death. I have used the word "parasite," which has a negative connotation, but we use the word "dependent" as a neutral expression when the activity pertains to people. Dependence is natural in the forest.

Sometimes the two organisms need each other to exist or interdependent. People are interdependent in a community. To different degrees, all are dependent on others. Our lives are not lived independently, although some people would so aspire.

Sometimes in life, we are more like the tree that is providing food, shelter, or benefit to others. We provide useful services to others through our jobs. But perhaps more commonly, we simply coexist with others. We are neither dependent nor helping others. Sometimes we can continue to simply coexist, or we can choose to engage our lives with others to be more interconnected than independent.

If we choose to use our time and talents for our own purposes, we may be like a fast-growing species that diminishes the diversity of the forest. For example, the black locust tree is a fast-growing tree that is very thorny as a young tree. It quickly creates a dense shade that gives it an advantage over other trees for sunlight. A young healthy forest can quickly be replaced by a pure stand of black locust because it shades the ground so completely that it reduces the diversity of the forest and the plants that grow on the ground beneath. But black locust trees are not completely bad—they put nitrogen into the ground which adds to the fertility of the soil, and they can be used for posts and firewood.

Oak trees also like to start in open areas and need sunlight to get started, but they grow much slower. They are of more value to the forest because their growth does not shade out all competitors, and they produce seed for the benefit of squirrels, turkeys, and other animals. Young oaks are not thorny like black locust, and their lower branches provide grazing for deer during winter. Oaks tend to provide better nesting sites for animals because they more commonly have hollows and stout branches. Although the black locust has value, to me the oak is a more desirable tree. Not only is the lumber superior, but the oak does more to enhance the forest ecosystem by providing for a variety of other organisms needs such as food, shelter, etc.

God has created our forests with a variety of trees, each with its own beneficial niche for numerous creatures. There is no one singularly important species; the variety is what makes a forest. The interdependence within the forest gives it great complexity.

Imagine a forest where all the trees are the same species and age. An even-age forest such as a thick growth of aspen has its benefits as well—it will, for example, make the ruffed grouse happy—but it is difficult to walk through. Variety and diversity is important for the long-term health of the forest and the interdependent creatures in it.

We each have our own unique gifts and talents. We enhance the lives of others as we make ourselves available to others and allow interdependence to occur within our community and enhance the lives of all involved. The parable about being a tree bearing fruit comes from Matthew:

> A sound tree cannot bear evil fruit, nor can a bad tree bear good fruit. Every tree that does not bear good fruit is cut down and thrown into the fire. (Matthew 7:18–19)

God calls us into community. We are to bear fruit to the benefit of others. Like different species in a forest, each of us has our own role to play. We have unique spiritual gifts and talents that may be used to the good of the entire community. Peter explains our interdependence:

> Practice hospitality ungrudgingly to one another. As each has received a gift, employ it for one another, as good stewards of God's varied grace: whoever speaks, as one who utters oracles of God; whoever renders service, as one who renders it by the strength which God supplies; in order that in everything God may be glorified through Jesus Chris. (1 Peter 4:9–11)

If we grow together with the strength of God through the Holy Spirit, we grow to a greater collective whole than what we would be if we lived independently to ourselves.

We find walking through woods more enjoyable if there are a great many species and diversity. Our spiritual forest will be more enjoyable for God to walk through if great diversity and interdependence exists. Embrace interdependence as an opportunity to give and receive in a community of interconnected lives. Our collective whole is greater that the sum of the individual parts.

CHAPTER 13

Hope

Ear-deafening buzzing shatters the woods. The noise silences the songbirds hidden by the few remaining bronze-colored leaves. A loud crack heralds the end of the buzzing, and the shadows above change position as if they are moving to get a better view. Limbs start to move, but there is no wind. Cracks and pops like the sound of expanding ice fill the woods and culminate in a thundering crash. Moments later, silence returns to the forest.

In the woodlands of the Midwest, walnut and oak are very desirable species prized for their lumber. They have wonderful grain and color. When walking through the woods, I prize the times I come across one these older giants. If left to grow, these trees can get to be three or four feet in diameter. A tree of this size may be over two hundred years old. Trees over thirty-six inches in diameter have become rare, as most of these trees are harvested before they reach this size.

When one goes down in harvest, it can be a sad thing to watch. Breaking limbs and a thundering crash as the tree falls, smaller, nearby trees often broken or damaged. Birds and animals previously dependent on the tree are evicted. But this process must happen for the creation of our furniture, homes, and a variety of wood products. Although I'm sad to see these marvelous trees cut, I enjoy admiring the color and wood grains in my furniture and other items made from these trees.

We have a dilemma. We enjoy the beauty and majesty of a great tree in the woods. Yet we recognize the utility of these trees to our society. There is a balance that we must walk between preservation and utilization. Here is a great controversy. What do we save, and what do we cut?

For now, let us conclude that complete conservation is just as unacceptable as complete utilization would be, and somewhere in between, we must find a satisfactory compromise.

When I walk the woods, I often find stumps of giant oak trees, cut many years ago. I look at the stump to see if I can count the rings or determine what kind of tree it was. Many stumps grow moss and become home to ground-dwellers like chipmunks, beetles, and lichens.

Sometimes I see hope. There at the edge of the stump is a rather inconspicuous twig with a few leaves at the top. It is a new shoot of growth from the old stump. Usually these grow out of the base of the tree just above the root line. New growth is a chance for rebirth of a great tree.

The book of Job shows the struggle for hope in the face of horrendous circumstances. Job has just lost everything, yet he looks at the hope of new life in the world around him and wonders if people have the same hope. You can hear the heartbreak in his voice as he speaks:

> For there is hope for a tree, if it be cut down, that it will sprout again, and that its shoots will not cease. Though its root grow old in the earth, and its stump die in the ground, yet at the scent of water it will bud and put forth branches like a young plant. But man dies, and is laid low; man breathes his last, and where is he? (Job 14:7–10)

Faith for man is like the freshly cut stump. There is the hope for a new tree, but for Job—and for us—there is the assurance of new life springing fresh in eternity. Job is restored at the end of the book for his faith, and his friends are scolded by God for questioning God's ways.

We also may have this assurance of new life when our life comes to an end. We may be like brand new shoots with a new "spiritual eternal body" fresh and vibrant but derived from the old. Just as cutting a tree is necessary, physical death is inevitable—but it doesn't have to be final. There is the hope for new life, a better life.

CHAPTER 14

Utility or Idolatry?

We were stuck in traffic, practically at a standstill. Looking around, we noticed a shop advertising Koa wood products. We decided to check the place out while we waited for the traffic to clear. Had we not been in that slow-moving line of cars, we would not have entered this shop on Kauai.

Intrigued by trees and wood, going in the store wasn't a difficult decision. We climbed out of the car and moments later were staring with great admiration at the wonderfully handcrafted wood objects on every shelf in the store.

The grain was fascinating—coarse lines traveling one direction, crossed by fine wavy lines in the other, all mixed together in a dark honey shine that marked the more valuable pieces in the shop. The more complex the grain, the greater the price tag. Burling of the wood created the complicated grains.

I wanted to buy a piece just to admire the grain and take it with me, but the fifty-pound bag limit for our luggage was on my mind. We left the store with only the memories of how wonderful the color of Koa wood can be.

Curious, I began to ask Hawaiians about the Koa tree. They explained that the tree grew at higher altitudes on the Hawaiian Islands. Koa is one of the surviving native trees on the islands, but it is being crowded out by the more numerous introduced species.

The next day we visited the Allerton Garden, the largest tropical garden on the Hawaiian Islands. This place was amazing. There was an expansive arboretum with trees planted from all over the world. As we walked, I read the name-labels placed around the tree trunks. Having seen Koa wood at the shop, I was on a mission to find a sample of the tree.

We walked for half an hour, admiring numerous wonderful trees. Eventually, we found the section of the garden devoted to native plants and trees. There, I noticed a young tree with somewhat silvery curly leaves planted inconspicuously along the edge of a garden. There on the tag was the name I had been searching for—Koa Tree.

I asked one of the garden employees about the trees, and he explained that the largest trees were mostly gone. They grow very large but very slowly and had been the early Hawaiians' tree of choice for canoes. The worker informed us that a canoe made out of Koa wood could be worth half a million dollars. He said that there was only one more Koa tree in the garden, and we stopped at the visitor's center to see it. It too was small, so I gave up trying to find one the size worthy of making a canoe.

Our flight was scheduled to leave that evening, so my wife and I enjoyed a pleasant dinner overlooking the bay at a hotel about a mile from the airport. As the sunset faded, we decided to walk around the elegant resort.

We marveled at large stone sculptures and two-story paintings that lined the entrance and lobby area. And then by chance, we found the most beautiful canoe we'd ever seen. We both stopped and stared at it with some disbelief. It was a solid wood canoe, nearly twenty feet long, and made out of Koa wood. It was made almost completely out of a single piece of wood. The canoe was finely crafted with the same fabulous colors and grains we had seen the day before in the shop. The finish was so smooth and well done, it pulled on your fingers to touch it, like the gravitational pull of a black hole. I could imagine how important a wood canoe would have been to the early Hawaiians.

Many cultures would carve or shape things with their hands and then worship them. The early Hawaiians prized the Koa wood for its use, but we cross over to idolatry when we place more importance on something than its basic function.

Isaiah 44:14–19 speaks against the making of idols:

He cuts down cedars; or he chooses a holm tree or an oak and lets it grow strong among the trees of the forest; he plants a cedar and the rain nourishes it. Then it becomes fuel for a man; he takes a part of it and warms himself, he kindles a fire and bakes bread; also he makes a god and worships it, he makes it a graven image and falls down before it. Half of it he burns in the fire; over the half he eats flesh, he roasts meat and is satisfied; also he warms himself and says, "Aha, I am warm, I have seen the fire!" And the rest of it he makes into a god, his idol; and falls down to it and worships it; he prays to it and says, "Deliver me, for thou art my god!" ... No one considers, nor is there knowledge or discernment to say... "Shall I fall down before a block of wood?" He feeds on ashes; a deluded mind has led him astray, and he cannot deliver himself or say, "Is there not a lie in my right hand?"

We are not to make idols of wood to worship; this is obviously ludicrous. But we may be tempted to make idols of other things in this world without realizing that we are doing so. For example, we may pursue money, possessions, power, control, beauty, or any other pursuit that consumes our energy and time to the point that it becomes a form of worship. We would do well to be able to walk away from these pursuits as nothing more than self-made desire.

Does my admiration of all things wood equal idol worship? No. Enjoying the simple wonders of our world is a good thing and is well understood by most people as simply "smelling the roses." Admiring a well-finished wood grain is one of the simple pleasures of our world. It can be similar to the pleasant sight of a flower. To touch the smooth finish of fine furniture is similar to smelling a rose. As an old departed friend of mine would say, "It's as smooth as a baby's butt." God created His masterpieces so that we could see and admire His great work. All of creation points to God.

On our trip to Hawaii, I didn't start out looking for a tree. But God placed Koa wood in front of me to ponder. I came home with the pleasant memories of this tree and its wood and the significance it had to native Hawaiians. Koa wood may be one of the most beautiful wood grains in the world—it's not an object of worship, but a marvel of God's creation.

CHAPTER 15

Remembering the Past

Twisted, gnarled trees all around, interspersed with flowers. Heavily beaten paths around the trees create clear spaces. The tree trunks have a circumference of up to the size of a small car but support meager branches with sparse, small, smooth leaves. It is not difficult to imagine these trees could be two thousand years old.

Olive trees, like many others, will keep sprouting new growth from the trunk when they're damaged or cut. For an abundant harvest, older trees are often removed and replanted with younger trees that bear more profuse crops.

But this olive orchard is special. This olive orchard has been preserved even though it is now enveloped by an expanding city. It no longer serves its original purpose of producing olive oil. This place is preserved because of what happened here, in the garden of Gethsemane.

The sketch for this chapter is the outline of one of those wizened old olive trees. I had barely enough time to take a few pictures, but my mind imagined what this place would look like in the dark or by lamplight. At the end of this olive orchard stands the Church of All Nations. Its windows are alabaster (cut translucent stone), and through one of those windows, I could hear the sounds of singing. It was a moment of sights and sounds not easily forgotten.

The word "Gethsemane" is the name for the pillar of rock that would be lowered onto a bag of olives to press them against a stone on the ground. The olives would be crushed under the weight of the stone to release the olive oil. Grooves were cut into the stone on the ground so that the olive oil would drip into the groove and subsequently run off into a collecting container. This garden was a place to press the oil from olives by using a great stone.

The garden of Gethsemane is where Christ engaged in a personal prayer vigil prior to His imminent crucifixion. (See Matthew 26:36–54.) Here He prayed to God for this burden to be lifted. In this place, His disciples had difficulty staying awake, and here Judas would betray Him.

Luke the physician is the only Bible writer who records one particularly interesting detail of this time in the garden. Luke 22:44 KJV says, "And being in an agony, He prayed more earnestly: and

His sweat was as it were great drops of blood falling down to the ground."

"Hematidrosis" is the medical term for sweating blood. It is an accepted medical phenomenon sometimes associated with disorders of the blood but also seen at times of great emotional stress.

The great weight of taking on the sins of the world and willingly going to His death without protest is Gethsemane for Christ. In this place used to crush olives into oil, Jesus allowed Himself to be crushed, to ooze the blood of sacrifice for all mankind.

This covenant of His death for our salvation is remembered in most churches as communion. When thinking of the past, don't dwell on personal failings. Ponder instead these great events of the past that allow you a life of freedom today.

CHAPTER 16

A Good Pack Tree

There are many tasks that need to be prioritized upon arrival at a wilderness campsite. The first order of business is to secure tent sites and put up tents to keep the gear dry. If you unpack gear before the tent is ready, you run the risk of sleeping bags and gear being soaked by an unexpected squall. Sleeping bags and pads must be placed in proper order and gear put away so that they can be located later when the party returns to camp at dark.

Other tasks that must be done include putting a pack in a tree, getting firewood, locating a privy site and getting it ready for use, preparing the next meal, and getting fishing gear ready. Setting up the privy may take precedence if the need to use it is pressing. Getting the fishing gear ready is usually the last priority.

Getting the food pack up in a tree is important in bear country. It is not a job that should be left until nightfall. Identifying a good tree and throwing a rope over a limb is difficult with flashlights in the dark. Carefully inspect the campsite and look for a suitable pack tree.

There are several characteristics of a place to hang your food. Obviously you must choose a tall, stout tree. Look for a limb that will allow the pack to hang approximately twelve feet off the ground, so that even the most ambitious bear will not attempt to reach it. If a tree has a lot of limbs, they may get in the way and make it difficult to throw a rope over the intended limb. Therefore, a tree with an open interior architecture and large branches is the most suitable site for hanging your rope.

There are techniques for hanging food packs that require the use of two trees some distance apart with two ropes. This may be a more elegant technique, but for me, finding one good tree is challenge enough. Finding two good trees the right distance apart can be very difficult. The ideal tree is very large with a singular, large, primary branch unobstructed by any smaller branches around it.

The branch that holds the pack obviously needs to be able to support a fair amount of weight. It would be best if the bark was smooth. Smooth bark allows the rope to slide freely up and down in its position, but it also allows for the movement of the rope down the branch, should the pack be too close to the tree. Rough bark may cause the rope to snag.

We generally have two large pines in BWCA canoe country to choose from: white pine and Norway pine. Jack pine, spruce, and birch are not usually suitable for this purpose. Norway pine, also called red pine, has a distinctive, puzzle-like flaky bark. This bark is more likely to cause the bark to catch the rope than a white pine. White pines are also far more likely to produce a stout lower limb, as Norway pines tend to do more branching at the top and their lower branches end closer to the trunk. Jack pines are also common, but are my last choice due to their rough bark, short branches, and sap covered cones. Getting sap on the rope makes for a sticky mess.

One final attribute that makes a tree ideal is when the trunk of the tree is positioned on a high ledge several feet above the ground. This allows the throw of the rope and pulley over the limb to be a short throw from the uphill side, but allows the pack to be many more feet off the ground if the branch is over the downhill side of the tree.

Once the tree is chosen, tie a pulley to the end of the rope to give it some weight in the throw. A single-wheel pulley would work, but each wheel cuts the workload in half. A double pulley is ideal because the weight lifted can be handled easily. A three-wheel pulley would make it easier yet, but the length of rope necessary to string through the pack on the ground gets to be quite long. A double pulley on the rope and a single pulley on the pack is a good compromise between the effort needed to lift the load and not having so much rope that it tangles.

For each of the campsites I use regularly, I can picture in my mind my favorite trees for hanging packs. My all-time favorite pack tree is at the east end of Tanner Lake, and it's pictured at the beginning of this chapter. This tree is a very large white pine. It has a large singular branch about a foot in diameter pointing toward the lake with almost no smaller branches. It sits up on a ledge eight to ten feet higher than the ground that lies beneath the branch. There are also several other trees nearby to which I can tie the rope. I usually choose a smaller tree twenty feet away to tie the rope to. The smaller tree allows me to direct the pack away from the trunk of the pack tree.

One rope suspends the pulley over the branch. A second rope goes through the pulley on the tree and a pulley on the pack to gain more mechanical advantage. As I pull the pack rope to hoist the pack, the rope goes through the arm strap to make it possible to pull the pack out away from the trunk of the tree. With a good pack tree, we can hang our food well out of reach and have it protected from bears in a matter of minutes. In a campsite with poor trees, however, we have sometimes spent more than an hour attempting to get a pack high enough in a tree.

A bad tree makes it difficult to throw the rope, and we often take turns trying to make a good throw. Occasionally, I have been embarrassed by a tree that had so many limbs that the rope got stuck. I once had to leave my pulley and part of my rope as decoration for the next campers to laugh at. For years I had laughed at the sight of rope in a tree, feeling the former campers were "rope challenged." Then I did it myself, and now I only smile in commiseration at the mishap that puts the food pack at risk to the bears.

Some scoff at the idea of hanging food packs at all. But if you spend enough time in the wilderness, sooner or later, the bears will find you. Once you have inadvertently fed the bears at your campsite, they have a tendency to hang around and come back for seconds. They are not particularly careful when raiding food packs or camp gear. We prefer to disappoint the bears to keep them wild. Even if you feed bears accidently, they will become habituated to people and our food, which increases the likelihood that they will eventually need to be destroyed.

I suppose that using a tree to hold my pack is far removed from the main functions of a tree. This use is not what most people think of when they see a tree. Some things can have purposes that were originally unintended or are beyond our ordinary expectations. Events may have unintended consequences that at first don't seem to be related.

Sometimes in life we attempt to accomplish one purpose but in the process end up accomplishing another. Suppose that you are planning a backyard party, and a large limb breaks off a tree. It lands astride both the neighbor's yard and your own. You decide to cut it up and keep the firewood for future backyard fires. Your goal was to clean up for your party.

It is possible that your neighbor could be upset because you took all the wood for yourself. But the neighbor could also be very grateful you cleaned up the mess. Perhaps you find out later that some difficulty prevented the neighbor from cutting up the limb themselves. They might see your help as a gift from God in a time of need. You may have had no intention of pleasing your neighbor, but cleaning up the fallen limb was received as a great kindness.

Good communication is vital to understanding your neighbors. An opportunity to help someone else may be the door that is opened to having a deeper conversation. Making a new friend, showing someone else that you care—these are ways to develop relationships that may bring opportunity for unintended benefits.

Many times helping others can be simply a matter of seeing something that needs to be done and doing it. Christian service is often like that. If we are honoring Christ in our lives, then we are serving others. We may be inadvertently evangelizing or serving God in a way we didn't realize. Wisdom, in part, is the understanding of greater purposes and unintended consequences. As God imparts wisdom to us, we learn of alternative purposes and the value of ordinary actions.

God calls us to be good stewards of our time, talents, and money. God wants us to share these things, not only for the good that they may do but also for the unexpected consequences we don't see.

Sharing the gospel are activities that cannot occur in the absence of some form of giving. Perhaps the original objective that we see as the most important is actually the tree on which another purpose is hung. The tree never intended to become a pack tree, but by being a successfully large tree with large open branches, it provided an unintended purpose. Consider what 2 Corinthians 9:11–15 says:

> You will be enriched in every way for great generosity, which through us will produce thanksgiving to God; for the rendering of this service not only supplies the wants of the saints but also overflows in many thanksgivings to God. Under the test of this service, you will glorify God by your obedience in acknowledging the gospel of Christ, and by the generosity of your contribution for them and for all others; while they long for you and pray for you, because of the surpassing grace of God in you. Thanks be to God for his inexpressible gift!

Our lives can be lived without purpose; without knowing why we are here. But wisdom comes when we find that we are living for other purposes that we were oblivious to when we were young. Unintended purpose in our lives may become our most significant purpose. Wisdom is the ability to see the greater purpose in our lives and in the lives of others. May our lives be like an old white pine—one that may be used for unexpected purposes.

CHAPTER 17

Take a Walk in the Woods

Our family takes many hikes in state and national parks. Some of the best trails we've found are the Iceberg Lake hike in Glacier National Park, Johnson Creek Canyon in Banff, and the teahouse hike at Lake Louise in Banff.

One day we chose to hike to Iceberg Lake. This hike is a typical park destination hike. We were prepared—our hiking boots, hats, cameras, lunch, and water bottles were packed and ready to go right after breakfast. It was warm and sunny with a minimal breeze—simply a great day for a hike. We started up the trail through a wooded draw and came upon a couple who were returning down the trail.

They obviously had not finished the hike because they did not have overnight gear. After a brief conversation, I ascertained the reason they were returning: they had spotted a grizzly not more than fifty feet off the trail in the brush ahead of us. I pondered this information while my family was catching up. I made the somewhat dangerous decision to continue ahead, but now we moved with much greater caution. I told the kids to make more noise, and I told them to sing. My eldest daughter would in future years take opera lessons in college, so I was pretty sure that a bear would hear us coming. We arrived shortly at the area where the bear was spotted, but we didn't see it.

We hiked several hundred yards past the spot and started to leave this low brushy terrain and head into a subalpine forest. We came to a bend in the trail where there was a great vista of the valley below and in particular, the area we had just hiked. Still thinking about the bear, I sat on a rock and scanned the hillside. I waited at this spot for the kids to catch up. Moments later, a dark form appeared several hundred feet below on the trail we had just crossed. It was low to the ground and looked like a large animal on all fours. I yelled at the kids to look at the bear. We were all lined up looking at it when another couple came along. They looked at it briefly and then took out a pair of binoculars. The stranger said "That's not a bear, it's a hiker." He handed me the binoculars in time for me to discern a hiker trying to focus his camera on a wildflower. My family roared with laughter.

They began to remind me of another vacation error where I stopped the car to pick up a pretty green rock, only to discover it was spray-painted. They would cry out, "green rocks!" anytime they saw anything remotely close to a green rock to commemorate my mistake. For the rest of the hike, I heard laughter interspersed with a few choruses of "It's a bear!" or "Green rocks!" These two things will forever have a double meaning to my family.

There are many things to do in a forest. Besides enjoying the inevitable trees and leaves, there are woodland wildflowers to find, animals to spot, and great scenery. There are many things to collect, including mushrooms, grapevines, deer sheds, and more. You can spend time hunting animals, hike for exercise, or use the time for bird watching. The one thing these activities all have in common is that the person in these various pursuits will find themselves traveling woodland trails.

Woodland trails exist for a variety of reasons. Some are trails that people make while walking to a destination such as vista, a lake, or a cabin. Some trails are primarily used by animals. Traveling animal trails in the mountains is dangerous, as you could actually come face to face with a bear. Animal trails also frequently branch, and while you might have started out following a wide, well-traveled deer trail, it can thin down to a raccoon trail and then to a rabbit trail and finally to a chipmunk trail that disappears into a hole. And you, my friend, are lost.

Traveling trails can be challenging and rewarding. When my son Eric was finally old enough to carry his own pack, we headed out on another family fishing trip. The portage was long and unused with several dead trees across it, but he made the portage without leaving his pack behind. This was a great triumph for him and a defining moment to adulthood.

Some trails I've enjoyed simply for the trees. Notable trails include the redwoods of California, and the trail of cedars in Glacier National Park. One of my favorite woodland walks was Lighthouse Park in Vancouver. Lighthouse Park was my first encounter with old-growth rainforests of the Pacific Northwest. Eastern Hemlocks and Douglas firs are truly spectacular on this small patch of land surrounding the lighthouse at the opening to Vancouver Bay. This remains the only old-growth forest in the Vancouver area because the lighthouse keeper refused to run the lighthouse unless the loggers left the trees uncut. I had not understood why old-growth forest is not a renewable resource until I saw it for myself. It would take hundreds of years to grow the forest back to this natural mature state.

There is one more activity that happens on a walk in the woods that is important to me, and that is the time I spend with God. Many times a walk in the woods is a time of contemplation. It is a time to think about the future but to be in the moment. There are times when a walk can be clarifying. Luke tells the story of a walk with Christ 24:13-17:

> [13] That very day two of them were going to a village named Emma'us, about seven miles from Jerusalem, [14] and talking with each other about all these things that had happened. [15] While they were talking and discussing together, Jesus himself drew near and went with them. [16] But their eyes were kept from recognizing him. [17] And he said to them, "What is this conversation which you are holding with each other as you walk?"

Two men walking from Jerusalem to Emmaus encounter a stranger who was actually the resurrected Christ. They don't understand at first, but the encounter made it clear to the men the significance of what they had witnessed (the crucifixion) and the promise of the scriptures. We may walk a quiet path and in the absence of distraction, find our thoughts are guided by the Holy Spirit. This encounter may shed light on the correct path for your life or show you the importance of certain people in your life.

There are more than leaves and limbs to study in the woods. There is life itself to reflect upon, to clarify, to understand, and perhaps to redirect. Live today, make today count, and understand the significance of the people and events in your life. Today is all you really have, so enjoy it, live it, and discern where your life path is going.

CHAPTER 18

Pillars of Faith

We carefully studied the map of the Lamar Valley in Wyoming. Finding the spot we'd planned to stop, we pulled off into an unmarked parking area. This particular parking lot was unlike most that we had found in Yellowstone Park. It was not paved. But the most striking difference between this parking lot and other lots in the park was the absence of any other cars. We were driving through the northeast corner of Yellowstone, enjoying the views of many herds of buffalo and other wildlife.

We had chosen to stop at this particular place because it was a trailhead to Specimen Ridge. On the many trips I'd made to Yellowstone since my childhood, I had seen most of the park. Specimen Ridge had never made the "to see" list, but I had always wondered about what was there. Several miles to the west of the ridge, there is a road where you can drive your car up to a single, solitary, fenced-off, petrified tree. There was once a trio of petrified redwoods there, but now only one of them remains. The rest have been carried off by looters and hikers, each wanting a piece of the tree. This one remaining tree is easy to get to, but Specimen Ridge had the promise of seeing more petrified trees.

We had seen the petrified forests of Arizona with their impressive collection of wood logs on the ground. We'd also seen the petrified forests of South Dakota. But the petrified trees of Yellowstone have a quality about them that makes them unique. More than one of the trees in Yellowstone Park have been identified as redwoods. There are several different species of trees found on Specimen Ridge—some of which are badly eroded, and some of which are well preserved. These trees have been left in their upright position, which is unlike most areas containing petrified wood. Most petrified trees are found lying down as a wash of logs, perhaps in the swamp condition where they became laden with water and mud and then were petrified with minerals.

The petrification process in Yellowstone is quite different than at other locations. These trees were standing at the time of a pyroclastic flow from a volcanic eruption and were buried in the standing position. A pyroclastic flow is not molten rock but superheated mud that flows down the volcano as an avalanche. In the wake of that debris, these trees were mineralized in their original location. In some areas the trees look like stumps where the tree had been broken off. Some had exposed roots still clinging to the surrounding rock.

⌇

We had no actual guide so we used a trail guide book describing the trail to take us to Specimen Ridge. We started up the trail according to the map, but quickly found ourselves confused by the various animal trails, including buffalo. The buffalo trails became more numerous and crisscrossed the hiking trail, making it confusing to determine which trail was the correct one. However, Specimen Ridge was apparent by the topography, and we continued to journey uphill in the general direction of the main ridge, hoping to find a more identifiable trail.

After hiking a good long distance from our car toward the tree line, I decided to stop and look back at the car to make sure that I could identify the correct path on our return. Suddenly I spotted a grizzly bear walking along a brushy, low gully several hundred yards below us and between us and our car. This was an obvious indication to me that we had reached the point of no return. We didn't want to walk back down the trail near this grizzly bear, so we figured we would go on up the ridge and after a couple hours of hiking, this bear would have wandered away from the car.

We continued to climb and eventually found the main hiking trail to the top of Specimen Ridge. The farther we went the steeper the trail became. As we neared the end of the trail, the rocks became loose, and slope grew steeper. My fear of heights caused me to slow down and walk with great caution. Cheryl, my wife, is less afraid of heights, and at times I found myself telling her to stay away from the edge because of my discomfort.

At the end of this part of the trail stood two large petrified trees and just beneath them, another smaller petrified tree. They stood as a trio on this hillside. These monuments of the past were amazing. We spent some time just enjoying the view and our accomplishment.

Petrified trees are like standing stones that mark the past, and just as the Israelites' standing stones marked great events, these standing stones mark a great calamity in Yellowstone's history. For me, it marked the destination. Some people see trees as simply a sign of the natural order, they see no evidence whatsoever of a divine Creator. But I would concur with the words of Isaiah 41:19–20:

> I will put in the wilderness the cedar, the acacia, the myrtle, and the olive; I will set in the desert the Cyprus, the plane and the pine together; that men may see and know, may consider and understand together, that the hand of the LORD has done this, the Holy One of Israel has created it.

Looking at a redwood tree that has been petrified by volcanic ash and subsequently eroded speaks to the marvels of this creation and the many wonders that we continually seek to understand. My hope is that these pillars will remain for centuries to come, preserved from looters and erosion as a testament to the grand redwood forest that once existed in Wyoming.

CHAPTER 19

Solitude

It is very common in Midwest and Western states to be driving an open road through vast countryside that is mostly devoid of trees. Then along the road or perhaps in an old fence line there stands a large, lone tree. It may be massive, left alone for years, and perhaps surrounded by cultivated fields.

Was the tree deliberately planted there? Was there a bunch of trees there before, and someone decided to spare only that particular tree? Does the tree mark the site of a rock or buried object to be avoided with farm machinery? Was it spared because of a child's tree fort or a bird's nest? Perhaps it bears the marks of lovers' initials or was the site of a first kiss.

Whatever the reason, a lone tree draws attention. It presents a focal point on the horizon. A single tree in the middle of a field draws our eyes to an otherwise barren landscape because it gives us a point of reference, perhaps a survival tool that we use instinctively.

If we take an anthropomorphic view of the tree, we might ask if the tree finds any advantage to being by itself? The most obvious benefit for the tree is sunlight. It can gather sunlight all day without interruption. It doesn't have to share water with trees; only the grass around it competes. Its seed has first chance at growing in the ground around it.

If we look at solitude, we find similar advantages. We have an uninterrupted view of the world around us. There's no distraction or competition from the crowd. We can be alone with our thoughts. We can have the time to reflect without worrying about a schedule. As in the game of chess, we have time to think through our various moves and options to see where they are likely to lead.

When Apollo Ohno suffered a setback in his short track-racing career, he thought about quitting. His father Yuki was upset because Apollo had seemingly given up. Yuki had made many sacrifices for Apollo's career. So Yuki took Apollo to a remote seaside cabin and left him there until he decided what he wanted to do with his life. After eight days alone at that cabin, Apollo called his father and said that he wanted to skate. It took time to solidify for himself what he wanted to do with his life. His decision to recommit to skating made all the difference. He developed into a short-track Olympic star skater.

In Exodus 3:1–2, God found Moses in solitude.

> Now Moses was keeping the flock of his father-in-law, Jethro, the priest of Midian; and he led his flock to the west side of the wilderness, and to Horeb, the mountain of God.

Then an angel appeared to him, and God spoke to him. It became a special place of solitude for Moses, a place he returned to, to be alone and hear from God on other occasions.

What does solitude have to do with making a decision or hearing from God? Using the tree analogy, there are no branches of other trees blocking the view or the sunlight. We can step back from matters of everyday life to see the big picture. We can clear our minds of decisions like whether to walk the dog now or take out the trash first. We can clear our minds of the clutter of TV shows, songs on the radio, or to-do lists.

Once free, we can reflect on what makes us happy and why we get up in the morning. We can dare to dream. Dreams are what energize us into action. If we don't dream, we are more apt to drift through life without goals, direction, or meaning.

Solitude does not have to be a rare opportunity, something to be found only in the wilderness or in a remote cabin. Solitude can be found in a quiet room, a drive in a car, or a walk down the street. Any time alone can be used to meditate or connect with God. Some schedule this time for themselves to make sure they don't miss out on it.

Prayer, meditation, or just being alone can be unpleasant for some. They may avoid it because they feel lonely when they're alone. They are sad because they enjoy the company of others. For some, solitude allows the mind to return to thoughts of past hurts that weigh one down and prevent optimism about the future.

Solitude can be lonely, sad, refreshing, or boring—but solitude has value. It may bring a defining point in our lives. Some people get a sense of what their life direction should be through prayer or meditation. Others may feel neglected by God because they lack clear direction for their lives. When solitude is available, be proactive and don't think about the hurtful things of the past. Past mistakes and conflicts are baggage we often carry with us. In the wilderness, it's best to travel light with no excess baggage. Concentrate on past blessings and the hopeful possibilities of the future.

Take a chance; clear your mind; search your own heart. When you are alone, without distractions, ask yourself the following questions:

Where is my heart?

What is truly important in my life?

What gets me really excited, motivated, and passionate?

Why do I get up in the morning?

Is what I'm doing and thinking going to matter two hundred years from now?

Would my best friend look at my life and honestly tell me to change something?

Do my emotions control my destiny? Do they prevent me from reaching my goals?

If I make a change, would that change make me or my family or my world better?

Ask the tough questions. If you are that lone tree, then you have an unobstructed view of the landscape. When you have the time to survey the landscape around you, focus on where you are and where you want to go. With a little prayer and quietude, God may direct your path.

CHAPTER 20

Taking the High Ground

Standing on Mount Haleakala on Maui at sunrise is one of the more celebrated things to do on a visit to Hawaii. The view is spectacular with steep volcanic cliffs falling away in every direction. Often the sun rises above a bank of clouds well below the peak of Haleakala. The native Hawaiians referred to it as the house of the sun.

Perhaps one thing that distinguishes man from other creatures is our desire for a higher viewpoint. We could speculate that our desire to hold the high ground and look out over valleys below stems from a latent desire for safety. But if we consider the amount of danger that exists in mountain hiking, we couldn't call it safe. What is it about a mountain view that draws us to build our houses so that they overlook lakes, rivers and mountains?

There are a few birds in the animal kingdom that will take the high ground too—using high tree perches from which to search out their prey. Mountain lions tend to prefer crouch on high, rocky cliffs or large, high branches to gain the advantage and surprise a deer or sheep below them. But no other creature other than man climbs to a high rocky ledge just to *ooh* and *ahh* at a sunset.

Very tall mountain ranges have tree lines. That is that point beyond which the conditions are so harsh, trees no longer grow. A few very remarkable trees will grow at this tree line or just below it with the ability to withstand severe extremes in temperature, water, and wind. The bristlecone pine that lives in the northern reaches of the Sierra Nevada mountains is one of the oldest living trees on earth. It grows very slowly, due to the harsh conditions in which it lives.

The advantage for trees living on the high ground is access to sunlight. In the dense forest, there is intense competition to reach the sun, and trees that fail to grow tall or reach the sun will soon die out in the shade below.

Many recreational activities center on high viewpoints—things like mountain climbing, skydiving, mountain skiing, and hiking. Much of the appeal of these activities comes from the viewpoints and the scenery that will be found while participating in these sports.

A tree sitting near a mountaintop would have the advantage over other trees seeking sunlight. And if trees had eyes, that tree would be able to see all the comings and goings happening below. Most likely, the presence of a tree at the top of a mountain is the result of a seed that was carried aloft on high mountain winds. When the wind stopped, the seed lodged in a crack with barely enough soil for it to take root. The seed didn't choose that location, but it was able to grow there. As the tree grew, it was subject to high winds, low temperatures, and sometimes drought conditions. But it persevered and grew.

As we trek into the mountains, we observe these trees surviving adversity, and we marvel at their contorted shapes. We may also find ourselves envious of their vantage points, at the sights that lie before them. Morning mists and sunset vistas seen through gnarly tree branches are often quite spectacular.

Many relish secluded, quiet, mountain spots as places for reflection and time alone. In scripture, we find Jesus Himself many times retreating to solitary mountain or desert places where there were few people and often a tremendous view. These were times when He had direct encounters with God.

In Matthew 17:2–8, we are told that Jesus took Peter, James, and John with Him to a high mountain place. Here, a most astounding thing happened.

> And he was transfigured before them, and his face shone like the sun, and his garments became white as light. And behold, there appeared to them Moses and Elijah, talking with him. And Peter said to Jesus, "Lord, it is well that we are here; if you wish, I will make three booths here, one for you and one for Moses and one for Elijah." He was still speaking, when lo, a bright cloud overshadowed them, and a voice from the cloud said, "This is my beloved Son, with whom I am well pleased; listen to him." When the disciples heard this, they fell on their faces, and were filled with awe. But Jesus came and touched them, saying, "Rise, and have no fear." And when they lifted up their eyes, they saw no one but Jesus only.

To commemorate the transfiguration of Jesus before them, Peter wanted to erect booths or structures of honor at the top of this mountain. Even today, mountain climbers who do not necessarily believe in God will erect flags or leave objects to commemorate their presence on the mountaintop. While in Israel, I got to visit the Mount of Transfiguration. While there, I too was seeking a mountaintop view, perchance a "mountaintop experience." I was disappointed to find that the top of the mountain is divided by a tall, impenetrable fence that separates the people of three religious faiths from each other. I spent much of the time that I had at the top of the Mount of Transfiguration seeking a view. Many trees were planted there, many buildings erected, but what disturbed me the most were those tall fences preventing access to different parts of the mountaintop. The best views were actually from below the summit, where the roadway dropped below the enclosures at the top of the mountain. I was able to get the view I wished to see as we left the parking lot. I hadn't really expected to hear the voice of God there, but I was disappointed in the lack of places to gain a thoughtful view of the surrounding countryside.

What is it that draws us to these high places, these places of danger and adversity, harsh places with amazing views? Is it a desire to be godlike and look down upon others? Do we desire a position of military advantage, to see the movements of the troops below? Or perhaps once there, the expanses below humble us into reflection?

Perhaps the most compelling reason is a sense of perspective; the realization that we are momentary and fleeting and the mountains we stand on are nearly eternal and more powerful than our brief lives. It takes time to think about the big picture, to think about our lives as a whole instead of the momentary. Perhaps in high places, we can reflect on the events of the past, but more importantly, there's room to ponder the future.

One future that we may ponder is what happens when we die. One of the tenets of Christianity that distinguishes it from other religions or from atheism is its concept of the afterlife. Afterlife is not subject to scientific testing. Afterlife must be taken on faith. Jesus clearly states that there is a heaven, and He tells several parables about it. But attempts to describe heaven in Revelation and other texts use worldly descriptions to describe the indescribable. One attribute of heaven that is particularly appealing is the idea that we will be in the presence of God. God is outside space and time and therefore is present everywhere and at any time throughout the universe. In Christianity, we do not become God in afterlife, but we would be in His presence. Being in His presence may mean that we have the opportunity to see what God sees. He sees the entirety of creation throughout time and space, and we would then understand more completely the events and lives that have occurred or will occur. When we read the account of Jesus' transfiguration on the mountain, He and the disciples are in the presence of Moses and Elijah. It is the deep desire of many people to be reunited with their lost loved ones. We hope that this is true of heaven, but we have no way to prove it. Some books attempt to provide proof of Heaven, but they all fail because the spiritual realm is not verifiable scientifically.

When we are on a mountaintop, we can see long distances. We get to experience many places all at the same time. I imagine heaven as the ultimate vantage point for space and time. Heaven is the ultimate mountaintop—both as a point of view and as an experience.

My challenge for you is to seek a mountaintop and let it transfigure you. Allow God's Spirit to touch you and reflect on your past. Allow the Holy Spirit to help you look to the future. Whether you're watching the sunrise on Haleakala, watching the sun go down on the Mount of Transfiguration, or simply looking out the window, God is there. Welcome Him into your thoughts and into your future. Carry that vision of the future with you.

CHAPTER 21

The Walking Tree

Walking trees can be found in many parts of the world. They are so named because of the large tuberous roots that descend from all sides, looking like many legs. These trees share several characteristics with the palm tree: they have smooth trunks with alternating marks where the leaf fronds attach, and the foliage is all at the top of the single trunk. Of course, the name is a bit misleading, because no tree can walk. Its "legs" are simply roots coming off the trunk above ground. These roots may allow the tree to be more successful in areas where water levels and rain amounts fluctuate, places like inlets and creeks.

If trees could walk, they would present a powerful image, like the Ents in the *Lord of the Rings*. In our human experience, trees are immobile. Wherever the seed or seedling is planted, the tree has no choice but to grow. If the seed fell in porous, sandy soil, it might die with the first drought. If the seedling is found at a high and desolate elevation, it could die from winter temperatures and wind. If it grows on shifting sands, it will likely blow away with the first dust storm. The tree that survives becomes a large successful tree, grown in good ground.

We humans aren't stuck in a specific physical location, but we are placed into a particular family. Therefore, our opportunities are often related to or influenced by that birth family. We are preprogrammed with a certain set of genetic codes, which on the one hand make us unique, but on the other can destine us to certain diseases. So, in a metaphorical way, we must grow where we were planted.

Perhaps economically, socially, educationally, and physically we are a product of our genetics and circumstances. These things may determine our starting point, but they don't have to limit our possibilities.

Even spiritually, the world does not look like a level playing field. God loves the world and freely offers his love to all for their salvation. But from our human vantage point it appears that not all have the same access to His word or opportunities for faith. God's judgment is true, and the judgment of a loving father. His judgment comes not as a tax collector to quantify your success. Not as a police officer to check your speed. Not as a judge at a beauty contest to judge your appearance. His is a spiritual judgment of what you've done with your opportunities. He doesn't compare you to others; He makes an examination of your heart.

In Matthew 13, Jesus tells the parable of the sower. It is a wonderful opportunity to understand scripture, because He interprets the lesson for His disciples in verses 19–23.

> When any one hears the word of the kingdom and does not understand it, the evil one comes and snatches away what is sown in his heart; this is what was sown along the path. As for what was sown on rocky ground, this is he who hears the word and immediately receives it with joy; yet he has no root in himself, but endures for a while, and when tribulation or persecution arises on account of the word, immediately he falls away. As for what was sown among thorns, this is he who hears the word, but the cares of the world and the delight in riches choke the word, and it proves unfruitful. As for what was sown on good soil, this is he who hears the word and understands it; he indeed bears fruit, and yields, in one case a hundredfold, in another sixty, and in another thirty.

We hope that we are good ground and that God will do the softening of the ground (our hearts). Many speculate on the spiritual judgment of others. They wonder how would God judge a Native American who lived after Jesus was born but had no contact with the Bible. Or what about a person born in another country, in an entirely different culture, and with no opportunity for exposure to the Bible. Many agnostics use this argument to prove that unbelief is acceptable, or they use it as a reason to wander into universalism. Atheists use this tactic to prove that a loving God does not exist.

Christians often conclude that a lack of knowledge about Jesus automatically leads to condemnation. This is based on a statement Jesus made when He was teaching on salvation. In John 14:6, Jesus said, "I am the way, and the truth, and the life. No one comes to the Father, but by me."

But God is the one true judge, and only He will make the judgment. For us to assume judgment for others is similar to playing God. This is not our job. Rather, we are to look to ourselves, to comprehend our own judgment. We will be judged by what we did with our own opportunities for a relationship with God. We may speculate on the opportunities of others, but we only have certainty about ourselves.

As for me, if I choose not to believe in Jesus, I condemn myself. In the parable of the sower, it is clear that we will be judged if we have received a "seed" of faith for a personal relationship with God. For those of us who have heard of Jesus, we are judged as to whether we chose to accept Him and to grow in that relationship. But let's not prove ourselves to be judgmental of those who have never heard of Jesus. Instead, let us trust God to make His true judgment and leave that judgment as a mystery. We have our own judgment to worry about. Those of us who have access to His word risk condemning ourselves out of our refusal of His invitation.

We have been planted in our culture, our family, and our community. Like a tree, we did not choose our parents or where we were born. Where we were planted can change our opportunities. What matters most is whether we accept what God has to offer us and what we do with our opportunities. Having been given love from our creator, do we honor Him by accepting His love?

CHAPTER 22

Standing on the Shoulders of Giants

On another family trip through the BWCA, we came to Iron Lake and found that it was very busy with other canoeists. We found the first two campsites fully occupied. The third was also occupied, so we decided to inquire of these campers whether they knew of any open sites. They indicated that they had also found most of the campsites to be filled, but they had seen one open site on the south side of the lake.

One of the campers said, "It's kind of hard to see and not very good, but it was open this morning."

I knew of a good fishing spot on the south end of the lake, so we headed that direction. When we arrived, we could barely tell there was a campsite there. If it hadn't been for a ranger-placed fire grate, I wouldn't have been able to identify it. The water was low, so we had to portage our gear across a muddy area to get to the small clearing in the brush. The location was so bad, one of the kids refused to get out of the canoe until it was final that this was going to be our camp.

We began looking for firewood, and I came across this birch tree in the sketch above. The tree had a strikingly elevated trunk with roots taking off well above ground. Unlike the tree in chapter 1, however, this tree had not formed this way because of erosion. There were no other trees around it with erosion and no creek or wash nearby. I think that this tree started growing on top of a stump or a log, which has long since rotted away. The new tree remains, growing two feet above ground level with its roots stretching to reach the ground. It is common to find trees growing on the stumps of other dead trees; this one was just interesting because there were no traces left of the former tree.

Our days are comprised of a continuous stream of knowledge, opportunities, and inventions that were made available to us by people of the past. Our scientific knowledge is the accumulation of discoveries by ingenious people of both recent and ancient history. Some of these discoveries were made by celebrated people, and others by people whose names have been lost to time.

Our legal system, literature, music, art, and virtually every category of life is carried on the shoulders of giants who have gone before us. Religion is similar, with traditions, teachings, and rules of living passed down over generations. Most religions are based on the revelations and wisdom of noteworthy people of the past.

In Christianity, this is true as well, through the Law of Moses and the teachings of the prophets. We stand on the shoulders of what they have written down as well as the teachings of the disciples. First Peter 1:10–12 explains:

> The prophets who prophesied of the grace that was to be yours searched and inquired about this salvation; they inquired what person or time was indicated by the Spirit of Christ within them when predicting the sufferings of Christ and the subsequent glory. It was revealed to them that they were serving not themselves but you, in the things which have now been announced to you by those who preached the good news to you through the Holy Spirit sent from heaven, things into which angels long to look.

It is tempting to throw out the Bible when we are faced with something in it that doesn't make sense or doesn't seem to agree with our personal experience. There are difficult passages of the Bible that some people use as reason to disregard the entirety of the text. The faithful have prayed for understanding through the action of the Holy Spirit to comprehend that which is mysterious to us.

When we were children, we were taught things as simply black or white. As we got older, we discovered unsettling changes to what we learned as children. For example, we learned that Columbus discovered America. However, as we got older, we learned that he actually discovered the island of Hispaniola and not the mainland. We also learned that the Vikings discovered North America centuries before Columbus, and may have traveled as far inland as Minnesota. The more one knows, the more complex things are, and the more questions arise. We find we often discover several more questions as we seek to answer one.

∾

If we receive the Bible in faith as the word of God, we can then benefit from the wisdom and knowledge it contains. If we see it only as a collection of stories, it will not be able to offer its wisdom and power to change our lives. We can benefit from reading the Bible if we approach it with the respect our forefathers gave it. This gives something in our lives that the Holy Spirit can build upon today to provide us a larger view of life and eternity. We can stand on the shoulders of those who have gone before us to gain a greater view of life and spiritual matters.

Reading the Bible can lead to questions that are difficult to answer. These are questions to be pondered. Searching for answers to spiritual questions leads to a richer life and greater understanding of what is important. This could be seen as a purely intellectual pursuit, but with Christianity, it is not necessary to understand all mysteries or solve all theological problems. Christianity is simply a quest to know the person Jesus Christ.

The greatest difference between Christianity and other religions is that Christianity is the establishment of a personal relationship with God. The Bible exists not as an end in itself but as a doorway to having a relationship with Christ as the triune God. God makes Himself personally available to us through His word and the Holy Spirit. Just as the birch grew from an elevated position of a former stump, we live with the advantages of the knowledge and wisdom of those from the past. We stand on the shoulders of those who have gone before us.

CHAPTER 23

The Tree of Life

I pointed to a large tree with smooth green bark and asked our Mexican guide what it was.

"It's a saber tree," he replied. He spoke at length about this tree native to the Yucatan Peninsula. The saber tree has several unique qualities. It gets its name from large thorns that are on the trunk and branches. It is a tall, straight tree with branches that come out at right angles. The Mayans referred to it as the tree of life. This tree held both survival and spiritual significance for the ancient Mayans.

The saber tree sends its roots deep into the underlying limestone. Much of the Yucatan has rocky or sandy soil, and in some areas there is no soil at all. Summertime heat is tough on life in the area. The Yucatan Peninsula is known for naturally occurring open wells called *cenotes*. A cenote is an opening in the limestone, perhaps eroded by water over time to the point that there is direct access to the underground aquifer. These vertical caves have fresh clear water at the bottom from rainwater that has percolated through the porous limestone and created underground lakes and rivers. Cenotes have been a source of fresh water for local inhabitants for centuries.

Cenotes held spiritual significance for the Mayans. They were indeed a source of life in an otherwise arid landscape. There is evidence that the Mayans sacrificed children of royal descent into the wells. Human sacrifice may have been brought to the Mayans by another tribe called the Toltecs. In another form of sacrifice, blood was spilled onto the ground to make a sacrifice for fertility of the soil. So the Mayans and Toltecs believed that sacrifices of blood to the soil would make it more fertile, and that sacrifices of humans to the cenotes would, in turn, bring about blessings for the tribes.

The Mayans knew that the wells were a source of life, as without the water they provided, it would not be possible to live in this region. The tree of life or saber tree was a marker of an underwater well or stream, as it could reach that water with its roots. Saber tree roots may go as deep as fifty to a hundred feet down until they hit water, but the tree gives evidence that the water is there. Much of the rest of the Yucatan is covered with more drought-resistant scrub brush and mesquite. Areas without water close to the surface could not support these large trees. So, early residents looked for the "tree of life" to find a place to live.

Saber trees had many uses. They tend to become hollow as they age, so the Mayans used them to make canoes. The branches of the tree come out at right angles and point in the four cardinal directions, and early Mayans would plant these trees at each of the four corners of their villages as a spiritual protection of life inside in the village.

Symbolically, the saber tree also represents the many Mayan gods. The tree is often pictured as having thirteen branches, each representing a god affecting life aboveground, and nine roots, each representing a god affecting things of the underworld. Some of the aboveground gods include the sun, moon, and Venus. There was also a rain god. The hollow trunk was seen as a conduit to both worlds and was thought to contain the snake god, the king of gods. Many world religions have various versions of the tree of life.

Trees do sustain us for life. They provide food, oxygen, shade, tools, building materials, shelter, and they are pleasant to look at. The Bible also refers to a tree of life in Genesis 2:9:

> And out of the ground the LORD God made to grow every tree that is pleasant to the sight and good for food, the tree of life also in the midst of the garden, and the tree of the knowledge of good and evil.

We don't know much about the two trees in the garden, but the tree of the knowledge of good and evil was the tree that Adam and Eve ate from. The tree of life may be a foreshadowing of Christ's crucifixion.

In a global sense, we depend on trees for our existence. We depend on them to provide oxygen, clean the air, provide habitat for other creatures, and provide us the lumber and paper and many other items we need for our daily lives. The early Mayans who inhabited the Yucatan uniquely understood the value of water and recognized the trees that marked the presence of that water.

More than just providing shade, the saber tree represents the possibility of life. Those who brought Christianity to the Mayans had some help in converting them, because the Mayans understood the idea of blood being a sacrifice to God. The crucifixion and crown of thorns may have also been more understandable because of their reverence for the saber tree.

There is much symbolic significance given to blood and water in the Bible. After all, we are human, and it is abundantly clear that these are things of great significance. Therefore, they also serve as useful metaphors. I think that trees are of great symbolic value as well, whether a saber tree or a crucifixion tree. We look to the cross of wood as a symbol of God's redemption, provided to us in Christ's crucifixion.

Unlike ancient Mayan sacrifices, Christians make sacrifices of money, time, talent, and praise to God. These Christian sacrifices are not made for the purpose of appeasing a vengeful God. Christian acts of service, prayer, or sacrifice are not about changing God's mind or trying to merit His approval. The Christian life is about being thankful and sharing God's grace with others. The Christian life is a celebration of what Christ has already completed.

Through the various trees of this book we have looked for spiritual truths. I hope that the next time you take a walk in the woods; you will be looking for God's knowledge and wisdom.

Made in the USA
Charleston, SC
28 April 2014